CW00642517

GUESS THE ATHLETE

Using the three clues provided, test your knowledge and work out who these sporting stars are...

ATHLETE 1

1. I have broken the world record in my sport 11 times.

2. I am the only athlete to hold all four major gold medals in the same event at the same time in my sport.

3. I was the first man to travel 50m in under 26 seconds, and 100m in under 57 seconds in my sport.

ANSWER: _____

ATHLETE 2

1. I hold the record for the all-time most career points (3,431).

2. I won my first of seven championships in 2008.

3. I am one title away from being the most successful sportsman in my sport ever.

ANSWER: _____

ATHLETE 3

1. I am Great Britain's most successful Olympic female athlete in any sport, ranked by gold medals.

2. I won the Team Pursuit and Omnium at both London 2012 and Rio 2016 Olympic Games.

3. I was appointed Dame Commander of the Order of the British Empire (DBE) in the 2022 New Year Honours.

ANSWER: _____

ATHLETE 4

1. I am a three-time World Champion, Olympic Gold medalist, and European Champion, retiring from my sport in October 2016.

2. I was appointed Dame Commander of the Order of the British Empire (DBE) in 2017.

3. I was the second woman, and the first British woman, to win BBC Sports Personality of the Year Lifetime Achievement Award in 2017.

ANSWER: _____

ATHLETE 5

1. I represented my country in London 2012 before turning professional.

2. One of my victorious fights in 2017 was named Fight of the Year by *The Ring*.

3. I am a two-time former unified world heavyweight champion.

ANSWER: _____

ATHLETE 6

1. I signed for a championship club in 2012, for a then non-league record of £1 million, before helping them win the championship two years later.

2. I hold the record for scoring in the most consecutive Premier League matches.

3. Within four years, I progressed from playing in the Conference division to representing my country.

ANSWER: _____

ATHLETE 7

1. I am the son of a former 1980s England cricketer.

2. I made my debut for Leicestershire 2nd XI in 2004, prior to my 18th birthday.

3. My name is on both Lord's Honours Boards, scoring a century in 2010, and taking two 5-wicket halls, one in 2012 and the second in 2013.

ANSWER: _____

ATHLETE 8

1. I am an England Women's full back, helping my country win the European Championships on home soil in 2022.

2. I moved to Olympique Lyonnais in 2017, winning the UEFA Women's Champions League in my first season.

3. In 2019, I became the first English footballer to win the UEFA Women's Player of the Year Award.

ANSWER: _____

ATHLETE 9

1. I was originally a 400m runner, however switched sports after failing to qualify for the national athletics team.

2. I won a silver medal at my first World Championships in Lake Placid in 2009.

3. I became the first British Individual gold medalist at a Winter Olympics for 30 years, after winning gold in Vancouver.

ANSWER: _____

ATHLETE 10

1. I have spent over 100 weeks at World Number One in my sport during my career.

2. I am the only British player, and one of only three players in the world, to win four majors by the age of 25.

3. I turned professional in 2007 and won my first major championship four years later.

ANSWER: _____

ATHLETE 11

1. I made my international debut in 1998, a year after making my senior debut for Newcastle Falcons.

2. I won 91 caps for England, reaching consecutive World Cup finals, and represented the British and Irish Lions on six occasions.

3. I retired internationally in 2011, as the highest point scorer ever for my country.

ANSWER: _____

ATHLETE 12

1. I made my senior debut for Crystal Palace in 1988 and finished my playing career with a club I managed the following season.

2. I have made more appearances for England as a manager than I did as a player.

3. In 2020, I became the first England manager to reach the final of any major tournament since 1966.

ANSWER: _____

ATHLETE 13

1. I am an English dual-code rugby international, representing England in Rugby League 11 times, and 8 times in Rugby Union.

2. I toured with the British and Irish Lions as a defensive coach in 2013.

3. My son has also represented England in Rugby Union, and my brother is an ex-English rugby league player.

ANSWER: _____

ATHLETE 14

1. I made my first-class debut for Somerset in 1974 and played at Taunton for 12 years.

2. I played over 100 test matches and 100 ODIs for my country, captaining in Test Cricket for twelve matches.

3. My most notable match contribution occurred in Leeds in 1981, in which I scored 199 runs and took 6-95 in the match.

ANSWER: _____

ATHLETE 15

1. I am the first female gymnast from Great Britain to win at the European Championships, World Championships, and the Olympic Games.

2. I competed in the Athens, Beijing, and London Olympics.

3. I retired from Gymnastics in August 2013.

ANSWER: _____

ATHLETE 16

1. I won six World Championships in my sport during the 1980s.

2. I was the first player to win all Triple Crown events in a single season, and I am one of only three players to ever complete this feat.

3. I lost to Dennis Taylor in the famous 1985 World Championship Final, which attracted over 18.5 million viewers, in a game that lasted 14 hours 50 minutes.

ANSWER: _____

ATHLETE 17

1. During my professional career, I won 15 WTA Tour Single Titles, including the 1976 French Open.

2. I hosted coverage of the Wimbledon Championships from 1993-2022.

3. I was famously known as a host of BBC's Question of Sport between 1997-2020.

ANSWER: _____

ATHLETE 18

1. I represented my country in seven appearances in 1967, before retiring in 1974.

2. My illustrious managerial career spanned 39 years, including 27 years at the *Red Devils*.

3. I have won the Top Division Title in England a record thirteen times, alongside five FA Cups, four League Cups, and two UEFA Champions Leagues.

ANSWER: _____

ATHLETE 19

1. I am a ten-time European Gold medalist in short-track speed skating.

2. I have competed in three Winter Olympics.

3. In the 2017 World Championships, I won world titles in the 1000m and 1500m events, as well as Overall Gold, being the first British and European Woman to do so.

ANSWER: _____

ATHLETE 20

1. I won a gold medal at both the 1980 and 1984 Summer Olympics in my athletic event.

2. I broke the World Record for my discipline four times, and won two Olympic, and three Commonwealth Golds, before being forced to retire in 1992 due to injury.

3. I won silver at the 1986 Commonwealth Games in the 4 x 100m relay event.

ANSWER: _____

ATHLETE 21

1. I was announced as the successor to Charlotte Edwards in June 2016.

2. I have represented England in 127 ODIs, 10 Test matches, and 88 T20Is, scoring over 5,500 international runs.

3. In 2017, I captained my country to a home world-cup tournament victory, beating India by 9 runs.

ANSWER: _____

ATHLETE 22

1. I am the second man in history to win long-distance doubles at successive Olympics and World Championships.

2. I retired from Track Running in 2017, before focusing on longer distance running.

3. I perform a famous celebration, raising my arms above my head to form a letter.

ANSWER: _____

ATHLETE 23

1. My highest grand slam finish is reaching the 2018 Australian Open Semi Finals, a tournament in which I beat 3rd seed Grigor Dimitrov in four sets.

2. I ranked as Britain's number 1 in 2018 and have reached as high as 14th in the World Rankings.

3. I was a member of the British Davis Cup team, the first British team to win the tournament in 79 years.

ANSWER: _____

ATHLETE 24

1. My older brother is the only athlete to achieve two Olympic titles in our event.

2. Alongside my brother, we were the first brothers to ever appear together on an Olympic Podium.

3. As of 2022, I am considered the most decorated triathlete in Olympic history, the only one to achieve three Olympic medals.

ANSWER: _____

ATHLETE 25

1. I moved over to the MLS in 2015, following 17 years playing in the Premier League.

2. I captain my country in two FIFA World Cups during the 2010 decade.

3. I was named Man of the Match during the historic 2005 UEFA Champions League Final, in which my club overcame a 3-0 deficit to win on penalties.

ANSWER: _____

IF THESE ARE THE EVENTS, WHAT IS THE YEAR?

Using these three sporting events, can you work out which year the statements are describing?

31 to have a go at, covering all years 1990–2020...

SPORTING EVENTS	WHAT YEAR DID THEY TAKE PLACE?
1. Manchester United become the first English side to complete the treble. 2. Lindsey Davenport won Women's Wimbledon Championship. 3. Michael Johnson sets new world-record in 400m in Seville (43.18s).	_____
1. Arsenal played their final game at Highbury on May 7th. 2. Italy won the FIFA World Cup; however, the final will be remembered for the actions of Zinedine Zidane. 3. Rafael Nadal wins his second French Open Title in as many years, with Roger Federer winning the other three Grand Slam Singles Titles.	_____
1. First Olympics to be held in South America. 2. Leicester overcame	

5000/1 odds to win the Premier League. 3. Denver Broncos won Super Bowl.	————————
1. Mike Weir becomes the first Canadian and the first left-handed golfer to win the Masters. 2. English Twenty20 Cup is first held, being the first professional T20 league in the world. 3. England win the Rugby Union World Cup, 20-17 after extra time.	————————
1. Two English sides competed in the UEFA Champions League Final, which ended in penalties. 2. Rajasthan Royals win the inaugural Indian Premier League. 3. USA win the Ryder Cup 16½ - 11½, to end the streak of three successive victories for Europe.	————————
1. Lizzie Yarnold won Great Britain's only Gold Medal at the Winter Olympics.	

2. Germany defeated Argentina in the FIFA World Cup Final. 3. Nadal wins a record ninth French Open Title.	_____
1. Brazil won the FIFA World Cup, hosted in the USA. 2. Commonwealth Games held in British Columbia, Canada. 3. Brian Lara scored 375 runs in a single day vs England in April, before later breaking the record for the highest first-class score of 501* for Warwickshire.	_____
1. Australia wins the Rugby Union World Cup. 2. Michael Stich wins his first, and only, Wimbledon title. 3. Super Bowl XXV is won by the New York Giants 20-19 over the Buffalo Bills.	_____
1. Sir Ben Ainslie wins his first Olympic Gold Medal.	

2. Los Angeles Lakers win their first NBA title in twelve years, defeating Indiana Pacers 4 games to 2. 3. Tiger Woods becomes the first golfer to win three majors in a calendar year since Ben Hogan in 1953.	_____
1. England win the ICC Cricket World Cup Final, defeating New Zealand in the final via a Super Over. 2. Tiger Woods returns to win the Masters – his 5th Green Jacket. 3. South Africa win the Rugby Union World Cup.	_____
1. Diego Forlan wins Golden Ball at the FIFA World Cup. 2. Graeme McDowell wins the US Open, ending a 40-year drought for Europeans at the tournament. 3. Winter Olympics held in Vancouver.	_____

1. Justin Gatlin wins his first Olympic Gold Medal, and in the same Games wins Silver in the 4 x 100m.
2. Best Mate wins the Cheltenham Gold Cup for the third consecutive time.
3. Arsenal completed the Invincible Season, completing the English Premier League without a single defeat.

_____

1. The Champions League took on its current name "UEFA Champions League", with Barcelona winning the competition.
2. England lose in the Cricket World Cup Final against Pakistan.
3. Summer Olympics held in Barcelona.

_____

1. Mike Tyson bites off a piece of Evander Holyfield's ear in the third round of their WBA Heavyweight title fight.
2. Tiger Woods wins his first Masters title.

_____

3. Athletics World Championships are held at the Olympic Stadium, Athens.	
1. Brazil win their 5th FIFA World Cup, defeating Germany 2-0 in the final. 2. Peter Ebdon beats Stephen Hendry 18-17 in the World Snooker Championship Final. 3. Commonwealth games held in Manchester, with England finishing second in the medal table with 54 golds.	_____
1. Stuart Broad takes 8-15 to help dismiss Australia for 60 at Trent Bridge. 2. Jordan Spieth wins the Masters. 3. Great Britain wins the Davis Cup.	_____
1. Chelsea defeated Bayern Munich after penalties in the Champions League Final. 2. Great Britain finished 3rd in the Olympic Medal	

Table with 29 Gold medals. 3. Europe achieved one of the greatest comebacks in Ryder Cup history by winning eight and tying one of the twelve singles matches, to win the cup 14½–13½.	_____
1. UEFA Champions League Final provided great entertainment, as Liverpool overcame a 3-goal deficit to win on penalties. 2. England won their first Ashes in 18 years, with Andrew Flintoff being named Man of the Series. 3. British and Irish Lions Tour to New Zealand suffered a 3-0 whitewash.	_____
1. Manchester City become the first Premier League side to reach 100 points in a season. 2. Alistair Cook scores a century vs India in his final Test Match.	_____

3. England reach FIFA World Cup Semi Finals, losing after extra-time to Croatia.	
1. England completed a 3-1 Ashes win down under. 2. Leinster beat Northampton Saints in the Heineken Cup Final to win their second title in three years. 3. Manchester United won their 19th English League Title.	_____
1. Ronnie O'Sullivan wins his first World Snooker Championship. 2. Lleyton Hewitt wins his first Grand Slam Singles title, and in the same year becomes World Number One. 3. Cheltenham Gold Cup not held due to the foot-and-mouth crisis.	_____
1. Steffi Graff wins 3 out of 4 Grand Slams, failing to win the Australian Open, in which Monica Seles	

was victorious. 2. United States wins 101 Olympic Medals in Atlanta. 3. Dallas Cowboys won Super Bowl XXX 27-17 over the Pittsburgh Steelers.	_____
1. Peter "Snakebite" Wright wins his first PDC World Championship title, defeating Michael Van Gerwen in the final. 2. Tyson Fury wins his rematch versus Deontay Wilder. 3. The Summer Olympic Games is postponed for only its fourth time in modern Olympic Games history, the previous three times due to war.	_____
1. England regained the Ashes, winning the series 2-1. 2. Ireland completed their first RBS Six Nations Grand Slam. 3. FC Barcelona win the UEFA Champions League, beating Manchester	_____

United 2-0 in Rome.	
1. Buster Douglas defeated Mike Tyson to become the World's Unified Heavyweight Champion, in a huge upset. 2. Nick Faldo wins his second Masters tournament in as many years. 3. Stephen Hendry beat Jimmy White 18-12 in the World Snooker Championship Final.	————
1. Phil Taylor won his first PDC World Championship. 2. Blackburn Rovers won their first Premier League title, denying Manchester United a hattrick of titles. 3. Pete Sampras won both Wimbledon and US Open Titles, both for the third time.	————
1. Australia completes an Ashes Series 5-0 whitewash over England, and later the same year,	

win the Cricket World
Cup.
2. Joe Calzaghe becomes
the first undisputed
super middleweight
champion.
3. South Africa win the
Rugby World Cup in
France, defeating
England 15-6 in the final.

_____

1. Grand National was won
by One for Arthur at 14/1
odds.
2. Australia defeated
England in the final of the
Rugby League World Cup
held in Australia, New
Zealand, and Papua New
Guinea.
3. Usain Bolt retires.

_____

1. Andy Murray wins his
first Wimbledon title.
2. Justin Rose wins the US
Open, winning his first
major of his career.
3. Miami Heat won their
third NBA Championship
Title, having successfully
defended their title from
the year before.

_____

1. Michael Jordan won his final NBA Championship with the Chicago Bulls, in a season known as the "Last Dance".
2. France wins a home FIFA World Cup, defeating Brazil 3-0 in the final.
3. Great Britain wins one bronze medal at the Winter Olympics in Nagano, Japan.

_____

1. Manchester United win the inaugural Premier League Title, their first league title in 26 years.
2. Shane Warn bowls the 'Ball of the Century' to Mike Gatting in the first Ashes test at Old Trafford.
3. The Grand National was described as the 'Race that Never Was', as the rave was void following a series of incidents, including starting tape malfunctioning, false starts, and horses failing to stop.

_____

MATHS QUESTIONS

Combine your sport and maths knowledge to solve these sporting equations.

Solve the equations from top to bottom...

KEY

X	Multiply
+	Addition
-	Subtract
/	Division

QUESTION 1

David Beckham's Famous Manchester United Shirt Number

X

Number of Olympic Rings

+

Number of minutes in one half of a Rugby Union Game

ANSWER: _____

QUESTION 2

Points awarded for winning the first two points of a tennis game

+

Runs awarded for hitting the ball over the boundary without

bouncing in cricket

-

Maximum number of rounds in a Professional Boxing Fight

ANSWER: _____

QUESTION 3

Score of one player in a deuce in Tennis

+

Most runs possible in a cricket over of six legitimate deliveries

-

Highest possible score with a single dart

ANSWER: _____

QUESTION 4

Number of goals scored in a hat-trick

+

Number of players on a Basketball team

ANSWER: _____

QUESTION 5

Number of events in a Decathlon

X

Number of games played to a win a tennis set to nil

ANSWER: _____

QUESTION 6

Number of Olympic Gold medals Sir Chris Hoy has won

X

Number of players in a Netball team

ANSWER: _____

QUESTION 7

Year of England's famous Rugby Union World Cup win

-

Points for potting the black in Snooker

-

Number of holes on a traditional Golf Course

ANSWER: _____

QUESTION 8

Number of points in Manchester City's 2018 Premier League

winning season

-

Number of minutes played in extra-time in Football

-

Number of points to win a singles Table Tennis game

ANSWER: _____

QUESTION 9

Perfect score in Ten Pin Bowling

+

Men's Javelin World Record Distance (*to the nearest 10m*)

/

Number of athletes in an Olympic Relay Race

-

Number directly opposite the number One on a darts board

ANSWER: _____

QUESTION 10

Number of balls on the table at start of a Snooker match

X

Men's 100m World Record Time (*to the nearest second*)

+

Highest Individual Test Match score in a single innings by a single

batsman

-

Number of Premier League Teams in the 2021/22 season

ANSWER: _____

QUESTION 11

Highest checkout in Darts

+

Number of points for a converted try in Rugby Union

+

Length of an Olympic sized swimming pool (*in metres*)

ANSWER: _____

QUESTION 12

Number of the 2016 Super Bowl

+

Number of runs scored in a cricket batting half-century

+

Distance of an Olympic Running Track

ANSWER: _____

QUESTION 13

Number of World Championships Michael Schumacher won

+

Number of games a single team plays in a Premier League Football

Season

-

Minimum number of darts thrown to win a leg of 501

/

England's finishing position in the 2018 FIFA World Cup

ANSWER: _____

QUESTION 14

Number of players allowed on the ground at one time from a

single team in Australian Rules Football

X

Number of Ashes Test Matches in a series

X

Goals scored by England in the 1966 World Cup Final (*including*

extra-time)

ANSWER: _____

QUESTION 15

Distance of a marathon (*to the nearest mile*)

X

Number of shots to score an Eagle on a Par 5 in Golf

-

Points achieved by potting all the coloured balls in Snooker

ANSWER: _____

QUESTION 16

Michael Jordan's famous jersey number

X

Number of Champion's Leagues Liverpool FC have won

-

Score for hitting the outer Bullseye ring in Darts

+

Highest break possible in Snooker

ANSWER: _____

QUESTION 17

Number of Grand Slam singles titles Roger Federer has won

+

Number of PDC World Championships Phil Taylor won

-

Number of Premier League titles Alex Ferguson won as manager

ANSWER: _____

QUESTION 18

Number of UEFA Champions League titles Real Madrid have won

X

Number of Ends played in Curling at the Winter Olympics

-

Length of a cricket pitch (*in yards*)

ANSWER: _____

QUESTION 19

Year of England Men's Cricket first ODI World Cup win

-

Number of points for scoring a 'slam-dunk' in Basketball

+

Wayne Rooney's famous Manchester United shirt number

ANSWER: _____

QUESTION 20

Number of times Red Rum won the Grand National

X

Alan Shearer's famous Newcastle shirt number

+

Number of Winter Olympics between 2000 and 2020

ANSWER: _____

QUESTIONS BY SPORTS

Find all answers from Page 149 onwards...

AMERICAN FOOTBALL

1. Which franchise is the oldest in professional football?

2. When was the first ever NFL match broadcast on television?

3. Which NFL team have appeared in the most Super Bowls?

4. Who has been awarded the most Super Bowl MVP awards, and how many have they won?

5. Which player has scored the most points in Super Bowl history?

6. What is the highest score combined in Super Bowl history (*both teams' score combined*)?

7. What name is given to the trophy awarded to the winning Super Bowl team?

8. Which four teams have never made a Super Bowl appearance?

9. Name the only player to play on three consecutive Super Bowl championship teams?

10. Who is second in the list of Super Bowl Championships as a player, winning two with San Francisco 49ers and three with the Dallas Cowboys?

11. Who won the first Super Bowl, played in 1967?

12. Which team did Tom Brady sign with in March 2020?

13. In which year was Payton Manning drafted, and which team picked him up as the first overall pick in the draft?

14. Which player holds the record for the most touchdowns in a career?

15. Which was the only team that the Jacksonville Jaguars lost to in 1999?

16. Who did New Orleans Saints beat in the NFC Championship in the 2009 season on their way to their first ever Super Bowl win?

17. Who holds the record for the most games played for one team, and what team did he play for?

18. What number did the *the Comeback Kid* wear for the San Francisco 49ers?

19. Which coach has won the most Super Bowls and which team did he lead to these victories?

20. Which team is commonly associated with a blue star?

ATHLETICS / OLYMPICS

1. In the 4 x 100 metres men's relay, which nation was the first to go under 37 seconds, and in what year did they achieve this feat?

2. Which woman won gold in the 400m Olympics in London, having also reached the podium in the previous Olympics in Beijing?

3. Who was the first athlete to run the 100m in under 10 seconds?

4. Which nationality were the three Women's 100m Hurdles medal winners at the 2016 Rio Olympics?

5. Which GB Heptathlete won Bronze in both Athens and Beijing, following the disqualification of two other athletes in Beijing?

6. What date was *Super Saturday*, the name given to the middle Saturday of the London Olympics, and how many gold medals did Great Britain win on this day?

7. Which countries have won the most Gold medals in the Men's and Women's 10,000m at the Olympics?

8. Which metal is the primary component of an Olympic Gold Medal?

9. Who is the only Men's Great British Gymnast to win three individual medals at three consecutive Olympics? Which apparatus did he win his medals?

10. Which three cities hosted the Commonwealth Games in the 2010 decade?

11. Who is the most decorated male and female GB Olympic athletes, ranked by total number of medals won?

12. Who is the only GB Athlete to win a gold medal at five consecutive Olympic Games?

13. Who is the most decorated Olympian in the world, and how many medals have they won?

14. Where were the first Modern Olympic Games held, and in which year?

15. Which was the first Olympic games in which all participating nations sent female athletes?

16. How many towels were required during the 2012 London Olympic Games, which lasted just over two weeks?
    a. 108,000
    b. 117,000
    c. 165,000
    d. 198,000

17. Which five colours make up the Olympic Rings?

18. Who was the founder of the Modern Olympic Movement?

19. How many countries have been present at *every* modern Summer Olympic Games? Which countries are they?

20. What age was the youngest known Olympic Gold Medalist?

21. Which year did the first ever Winter Olympics take place?

22. Which nation has won the most Winter Olympic Gold Medals since its inception?

23. Which was the first Olympic Games to be broadcasted on television?

24. Which event are the world records: 74.08m for Men and 76.80m for Women?

25. Which event is GB athlete Colin Jackson most associated with?

26. Name the four men that won Gold Medals at the 2000 Sydney Olympics in the Coxless Four?

27. Which cycling event was first introduced into the Beijing 2008 Olympics?

28. What was the name of Torvill and Dean's Gold medal-winning, and perfect six-scoring, performance?

29. What height is the Olympic Large Hill Ski Jump slope, being consistent since the 1992 Winter Games?

30. Which athlete is the most successful GB Winter Olympian, and in which event did they compete?

BASKETBALL

1. In which Olympic Games did the USA's *Dream Team* compete?

2. Which coach has won the most World Championships, and which two teams has he won the championship with as a coach?

3. Which player holds the record for the most points scored in an NBA season?

4. Which player has scored the most points in a career?

5. Which team has won the most NBA Championships?

6. Which team was the first to win consecutive NBA Championships?

7. Which team won their first NBA Championship in 2016, after trailing the series 3-1?

8. Which team did LeBron James win his first two NBA Championships with?

9. Which team has the best NBA season record, and in which season?

10. Who holds the record as the youngest player to be drafted, and youngest player to debut in NBA history?

11. Who has won the most NBA Finals MVPs?

12. Which year was Kobe Bryant drafted, and which team was he selected by?

13. Who is the only other player to win the NBA All-Star Game MVP award a record four times, a record shared with Kobe Bryant?

14. Which player won All-Star Game MVP, NBA MVP, and NBA Finals MVP awards in 2000?

15. What shirt number did Michael Jordan wear when he returned to the NBA in 2995, before switching back to his most famous number following a first game defeat in the Playoffs?

16. Which NBA team plays at Madison Square Garden?

17. Which team holds the record for most consecutive NBA Championship Titles, and how many did they win in a row?

18. Which team swept the NBA Finals, beating Cleveland Cavaliers 4-0 in the 2007 series?

19. Who holds the record for the most points in a playoff game, and how many did he score?

20. What is the name of Golden State Warrior's arena, which opened in September 2019?

BOXING

1. What name is given to the famous fight between Muhammad Ali and George Foreman on October 30th, 1974, and which country was it held in?

2. What round did Anthony Joshua beat Wladimir Klitschko in on the 29th April 2017 at Wembley Stadium?

3. What term is given to a boxer who holds all titles from the four major sanctioning organizations – WBA, WBC, IBF, WBO – at the same time?

4. Which weight class falls between Lightweight and Heavyweight, in the Traditional Weight division?

5. Which boxer has won the most world championships in the greatest number of glamour divisions?

6. Which fighters fought in the *Fight of the Century* in 1971?

7. Which Welsh fighter retired in 2008, with a record of 46 wins (32 by KO), 0 draws, 0 losses?

8. Who won the *Money Fight* in August 2017 between Floyd Mayweather Jr. and Conor McGregor?

9. How old was George Foreman when he became the oldest heavyweight champion?

10. Nicola Adams retired from Professional boxing in 2019, with an undefeated record in which weight division?

11. Who did Anthony Joshua suffer his first defeat of his career to in Madison Square Garden in New York?

12. Which Olympic Games did Amir Khan win silver for Great Britain in the Lightweight division?

13. Which city did Deontay Wilder vs Tyson Fury II take place in, on February 22nd 2020?

14. Which Hull-born, lightweight professional boxer won gold for Great Britain in the 2012 Olympics?

15. Which is the northern-most UK city that Anthony Joshua has fought in?

16. In which weight division did David Haye become a Unified World Champion in 2008, winning 3 of the 4 major world titles?

17. Which fighter is responsible for Sugar Ray Leonard's first career defeat?

18. What was Muhammad Ali's birth name?

19. Who holds the record for being the youngest heavyweight boxer to win a heavyweight title, at 20 years 4 months and 22 days old?

20. What record did Floyd Mayweather Jr. retire with, after his one-fight-comeback against McGregor in 2017?

CRICKET

1. What is the cumulative series score for all matches played in the Ashes since the start of the 2005 Ashes until the end of the 2019 series?

2. Which bowler is the fastest to reach 300 Test Wickets?

3. Which batsmen is the fastest to reach 10,000 test match runs (*by matches played*)?

4. What is the highest ODI team score, and which nation scored it?

5. Which Australian Big Bash team won their first title in the 2019/20 tournament, after being runners up in both the 2014/15 and 2016/17 competition?

6. How many wickets did England require on 7th August 2005 at Edgbaston to win the test match and level the series 1-1, before later winning the Ashes for the first time in 18 years?

7. How many balls did Jack Leach face in his heroic innings at Headingley 2019, whilst contributing 1 run in a 76 last-wicket partnership with Ben Stokes?

8. Name the last 3 players to captain an ODI for England?

9. Which county has won the England Men's Twenty20 competition the most times?

10. Which player scored the most runs in the 2017 Women's One Day World Cup?

11. Which three teams did England lose to on their way to winning the ICC 2019 Cricket World Cup?

12. Who was the second top scorer, and supporting role, in the England innings, whilst Ben Stokes scored his Test Match high score of 258 vs South Africa in 2016?

13. Who was the leading run scorer in the 2019 ICC Cricket World Cup?

14. Which player scored the third most runs in the tournament, and took 11 wickets at the ICC 2019 World Cup, despite his team not qualifying for the semi-finals?

15. Who captained England to their first Ashes Test Series win for 18 years, in 2005?

16. Which year was the first Ashes series played between England and Australia?

17. Which player was the leading run scorer in the 2013 Ashes series, scoring 562 runs at an average of 62.44, having previously played in four Ashes series?

18. Which IPL team did Sam Curran sign for in the 2018 tournament, receiving the third highest auction bid value at 72m rupees (*£800,000*)?

19. Which two batsmen share the record for the most runs scored in a career-partnership together in test cricket?

20. Which two England players played in the Big Bash 2018/19, IPL 2019, 2019 ICC World Cup, and the 2019 Ashes?

CYCLING

1. How many stages make up the modern edition of the Tour De France?

2. What name is given to the Track cycling event in which two individuals compete against each other, starting at opposite sides of the velodrome?

3. Which two Great British Track cyclists have won six Olympic Gold Medals each?

4. Name the three *Grand Tours* in cycling, all following similar formats of three weeks racing split into stages?

5. In what year was the first Tour De France held?

6. What colour jersey is presented to the Overall Leader of the General Classification at the Tour De France?

7. Who would wear the White Jersey during the Tour De France?

8. Which Great British rider won a bronze Olympic medal in the same year as winning the Tour De France?

9. Greg LeMond retired from professional racing in December 1994, having been considered one of the greatest American riders of all-time. How many times did he win the Tour De France?

10. The Milan – San Remo cycling event, also known as *La Primavera*, is renowned for being a sprinter's race despite being on of the longest single day bike races. Which sprinter from the Isle of Man won it in 2009?

11. Which rider holds the record for the most Grand Tour victories?

12. What is the only year in which the three Grand Tours have been won by three different Great British cyclists?

13. How many stages comprise the Tour of Britain, having increased to this number in 2008?

14. The five oldest, longest and most prestigious one-day races in professional cycling are grouped together under what name?

15. Which event did Chris Hoy win an Olympic Gold Medal in at the 2008 Olympics, however failed to repeat the feat in London 2012?

16. How many Tour De France titles were won by Team Sky during the 2010 decade?

17. Which nationality was the 2019 Tour De France winner, Egan Bernal, who won both the overall classification and the young rider classification?

18. Which country has won the most Gold Medals at the UCI Road World Championships?

19. Which country was host to the 2019 UCI Road World Championships, which took place between 22nd and 29th September?

20. What was the first cyclist to win the Vuelta a España three times in a row?

DARTS

1. Which famous venue hosts the PDC World Championships, having been the venue for the event since December 2007?

2. Who holds the record for the highest PDC World Championship one-match average?

3. What nickname is the 2019 PDC World Champion most commonly known by?

4. Who was the first woman to win a match, and subsequently two consecutive matches, at the PDC World Championships beating Ted Evetts 3-2 in the first round, and Mensur Suljović 3-1 in the second round, before losing to Chris Dobey in round three?

5. Which player did Phil Taylor beat to win his first World Championship title?

6. What is the highest possible checkout in a standard darts game?

7. In which year did Rob Cross beat Phil Taylor to win the PDC World Championship, having just turned professional 11

months prior to the event?

8. Who did Eric Bristow beat in the 1980 World Championship final to secure his first title and start a decade's worth of domination?

9. Keither Deller defeated Eric Bristow by 6 sets to 5 in the final of the BDO World Championships in 1983 by successfully completing a high checkout, which has become synonymous with his name. What score did Deller checkout to win the deciding set?

10. In what year did several players, including Phil Taylor, form the World Darts Council (WDC), which later became the PDC?

11. In the 2010 Premier League Darts final, Phil Talor became the first player to hit two 9-dart finishes in the same game. Who was the victim of this feat?

12. Which betting company sponsored the PDC World Championships between 2003-2014?

13. Which Canadian darts player was the only other player than Phil Taylor to win the PDC World Championship between 1995-2006, and in which year did he beat *The Power*?

14. To complete a checkout of 161 in three darts, what target would a player have to hit with their third dart?

15. Which English darts player won the BDO World Championships for three consecutive years between 2017-2019, and then reached the quarter finals of the PDC World Championship the following year?

16. Which darts player was fined and given a 3-month suspension following his behaviour in the Grand Slam of Darts 2019 Final against Gary Anderson?

17. With which three letters is the winner of the PDC World Championships in 2014, 2017, and 2019, most commonly known by?

18. What name is given to the tournament in which players from the BDO are invited to face off against the PDC top players, the tournament which Phil Taylor won the first three years in 2007-2009?

19. Which PDC darts referee is known as *The Voice*, due to his distinctive and unique calling style, being the caller when Phil Taylor hit the PDC's first=ever televised nine-dart in 2002?

20. Who did Michael Van Gerwen beat in the 2018 Premier League of Darts Final to reach his fourth Premier League title, before adding another title the following year?

FOOTBALL

1. What minute did Sergio Aguero score to win the title for Manchester City vs QPR in 2012? What score did the game finish?

2. Which year was the first English Premier League season competed, and who won the title?

3. Which six teams have never been relegated from the English Premier League?

4. In the 2014 FIFA World Cup Final, which player broke the deadlock in extra time to win his nation's fourth World Cup?

5. Which two English players have won the World Cup Golden Boot?

6. Which goalkeeper holds the record for longest time without conceding a goal in the Premier League, and how many consecutive clean sheets did he keep?

7. Which three players shared the 2018-19 Premier League Golden Boot?

8. Name the world record transfer for each of the following positions: *Goalkeeper; Defender; Midfielder; Forward.*

9. Which three countries will the 2026 FIFA World Cup be hosted across?

10. Which was the first UK team to win the European Cup?

11. What name was given to the 2010 FIFA World Cup Ball, most famously known for its excessive movement through the air?

12. Which player joined Liverpool in 31st January 2011, for a £22.8 million fee, scoring on his debut two days later, before going on to score 69 goals for the club in four seasons?

13. Which team completed the domestic treble in the 2018/19 season, beating Chelsea on penalties to secure the EFL Cup, and Watford comprehensively to win the FA Cup?

14. Which country entered 2016 as the Number One ranked football team in the world?

15. Which English team has won the European Cup more times than the English Top Division?

16. What nationality was the Real Madrid attacking midfielder, who won the 2014 FIFA World Cup Golden Boot?

17. On 8th March 2017, Barcelo reversed a four-goal deficit from the first legs to beat PSG 6-1 (6-5 on aggregate) and progress to the UEFA Champions League Quarter Finals. Three goals were scored from the 88th minute onwards, but which player scored the 6th goals for Barcelona in the 95th minute?

18. Which team is the most northerly in the English Football Leagues?

19. Which player won the Football Writer's Association Footballer of the Year Award, the PFA Fan's Player of the Year Award, and the Football Supporter's Federation Player of the Year Award in the 2017/18 season?

20. Which manager has managed the most clubs in the Premier League? Can you name all seven?

FORMULA ONE

1. Which team did Sebastien Vettel race for during four consecutive World Driver's Championship victories between 2010-2013?

2. Who was the last British Formula One World Champion in the 20th century, and in which did he win it?

3. Who was the oldest winner of the World Driver's Championship?

4. Which circuit has hosted the most Formula One Grand Prix races?

5. Which Formula One constructor, created by a management buyout of Honda in 2009, won their first and only Constructors Championship in their only season of racing?

6. Kimi Räikkönen won his only Formula One title in which year?

7. Which year did Michael Schumacher win his first, of seven, Formula One World Driver's Championships?

8. The 2016 Formula One season saw the grid expand to twenty-two cars, with the addition of which racing team?

9. Which team did Lewis Hamilton win his first Formula One World Driver's Championship with?

10. Which nationality of drivers won the most Driver's Championships between 2000-2010?

11. Who was the first, and only French winner of a World Driver's Championship, winning his first of four titles in 1985?

12. In which year were Pit Stops introduced into Formula One Racing, allowing drivers to refuel mid-race?

13. Who finished as a runner-up to Jenson Button in the World Driver's Championship in 2009?

14. Which team have won the most Constructor's Championships in history?

15. In 2003, who became the youngest driver to be in pole position at Malaysia, and later the same year, became the youngest Grand Prix race winner at Hungary?

16. In the 2015 Malaysian Grand Prix, who became the youngest driver to score points in Formula One history?

17. Can you identify this circuit?

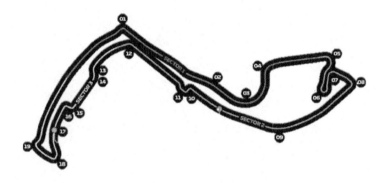

18. Can you identify this circuit?

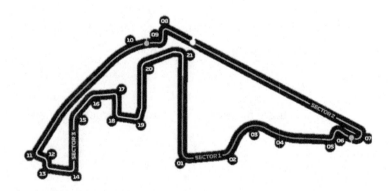

19. Can you identify this circuit?

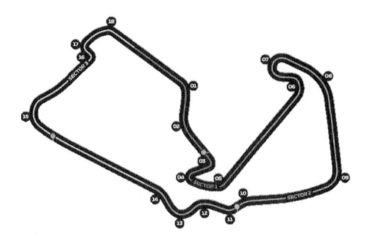

20. Can you identify this circuit?

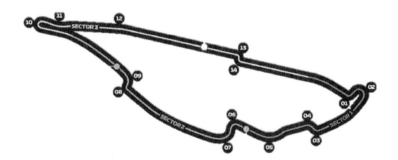

GOLF

1. As of the 1st January 2022, which is the only major Rory McIlroy has failed to win?

2. What name is given to the trophy presented to the winner of The Open Championship?

3. Which American won his first of two Masters Titles in 2012, despite failing to carry the form over into other major events, having yet to win another major title?

4. In the year 2000, Tiger Woods won his third, fourth and fifth major titles. Which Major did he fail to win this year?

5. Which two golfers struck up a relationship labelled *"Moliwood"*, following great success in the Ryder Cup together?

6. Which player won back-to-back U.S Open Championships in 2017 and 2018, and repeated the feat by winning back-to-back PGA Championships in 2018 and 2019?

7. Who, nicknamed "The King", became the youngest Ryder Cup winning captain in 1963, at 34 years and 31 days?

8. At which course has the Masters Tournament been held every year since 1932?

9. Name the only non-American player to win a major in 2015, winning his Major scoring a record 20 under par?

10. In which year did Nick Faldo win his first Major event?

11. What nationality is three-time Major winning, Vijay Singh?

12. Who became the first English player to win a major since Nick Faldo, and which major did he win?

13. Which course has hosted The Open Championship more times than any other, being used 29 times?

14. Which trophy is contested between amateur women golfers from the U.S and Europe & Ireland?

15. Who was the first non-American winner of the Masters, in 1961?

16. Who did Sergio Garcia beat in a playoff to win his first Masters in 2017?

17. How many points is required for a team to win the Ryder Cup?

18. What is the maximum number of clubs allowed in a player's golf bag?

19. Which Irish golfer won consecutive Open Championships in 2007 and 2008?

20. Which golfer finished in the Top 10 in all four majors in the 2014 season, despite not winning a title that year?

HORSE RACING

1. Which is the only other horse to win consecutive Grand Nationals, repeating the feat set by Red Rum in 1973 and 1974?

2. There have been two horses in the 21st Century to win the Grand National after having a starting price greater than 50/1. A 66/1 winner in 2013, and 100/1 winner in 2009. Can you name them?

3. In what year did Frankie Dettori complete the magnificent 7 and ride all seven winners at the card at Ascot?

4. How long is a furlong in metres?

5. Who won the Cheltenham Gold Cup in 2018, after finishing in 3rd place the previous year?

6. Which racecourse hosts the yearly Grand National horse race?

7. Who trained the 2010 Grand National winner Don't Push It (10/1JF), and then two years later trained Synchronised to win the Cheltenham Gold Cup?

8. How many winners did Willie Mullins train at the 2015 Cheltenham Festival, a record later equaled by Gordon Elliot in 2018?

9. The trainer of one of the greatest runners of all time, Red Rum, also trained the 2004 Grand National winner, Amberleigh House. Who is this trainer?

10. At which course is the Celebration Chase run?

11. How many times did jockey Lester Piggot win the Epsom Derby?

12. Which jockey won back-to-back Grand Nationals in 2014, on Pineau de Re, and in 2015, on Many Clouds?

13. Who finished as runner up to Tiger Roll in the 2018 Grand National?

14. Which horse is next in this sequence:
    Ballabriggs → *Neptune Collonges* → *Auroras Encore* → ?

15. Who is the most recent jockey to win the Grand National at his first attempt?

16. The British Classics are five long-standing Group 1 horse races run during the traditional flat racing season. Which race, at present, is the first to be run in the year?

17. Which horse completed a hat-trick of wins at the Ascot Gold Cup, winning the race in 2018, 2019, and 2020?

18. How many fences are jumped to complete the Grand National?

19. Which horse finished second in the 2018 Cheltenham Gold Cup, before winning the Betway Bowl Chase at Aintree, a month later?

20. Which company has sponsored the Grand National since 2017?

RUGBY UNION

1. Which two international teams has Eddie Jones coached to Rugby Union World Cup Finals?

2. Who scored England's only try in the 2003 Rugby World Cup Final?

3. In International Rugby, who is the all-time leading points scorer?

4. What name is given to the trophy won by the victorious team between England and Ireland, as part of the Six Nations?

5. Which country has completed the most Grand Slams in the Six Nations, and how many have they won?

6. Which duo was appointed coach and captain for both the 2013 and 2017 British & Irish Lions Tours?

7. Which team won the 2010 Six Nations, and the following year reached the World Cup Final?

8. Which are the only two teams to win a home World Cup?

9. Who did Jonny May score his first international test hat-trick against on 10th February 2019, inside 30 minutes?

10. Who did South Africa beat in the 2019 World Cup Sem-Final, on their way to winning the trophy?

11. Which Welsh fly-half was the first player to score more than 1,000 international points?

12. Which team won the most Premiership Rugby titles during the 1990s?

13. Which team defeated Wasps in the Premiership Final after extra-time in the 2016/17 season?

14. Which year did the English domestic top division change so that the winner was determined by winning a Premiership Final, rather than finishing top of the league?

15. Which Premiership team did George Ford move to in 2013, representing for four seasons, before returning to his first club, Leicester Tigers?

16. Which Premiership club has won the most titles?

17. Which year did the Five Nations become the Six Nations, and which country joined the competition?

18. Which Italian player holds the record for the most appearances in the Six Nations?

19. Announced on 7th December 2018, which company became the Six Nation's new title sponsor?

20. Which two teams share the record for the most European Champions Cup (Heineken Cup) titles, at four each?

SNOOKER

1. In which city is the famous Crucible Theatre, home to the World Snooker Championships since 1977?

2. Who has won the World Snooker Championship the most times, and how many times has he won it?

3. Which Welsh player defeated Mark Selby in the opening round of the 2018 Masters Tournament, a reversal of the opening round the year before?

4. Which Australian won the World Championship in the 2009/10 season, and following it up by winning the Masters two years later, beating Shaun Murphy 10-6 in the final?

5. Which Scottish player did Ronnie O'Sullivan beat in the final to win his first World Championship title?

6. Who was nicknamed "The Whirlwind"?

7. In which season did the Alexandra Palace first host the Masters, previously being held at Wembley Area for five previous seasons?

8. Who, as an underdog, beat Steve Davis 18-12 in the 1986 World Snooker Championship Final, and the following year reached the final again?

9. Mark Williams won his first World Championship title in 2000. Who was the last Welshman before him to have won it?

10. Which player has reached the Champion of Champions Final twice, first in 2014, and then later in 2019, despite not winning either final?

11. What national was 1983, 1985, and 1986 Masters Winner, Cliff Thorburn?

12. Which year did Steve Davis win his first World Championship?

13. In which year did Peter Ebdon turn to professional snooker, making an immediate impact by beating Steve Davis in the first round of the World Championships the following year?

14. How many times did Jimmy White lose in the World Championship Final?

15. Which company sponsored the World Snooker Championship between 2009-2012, and later re-sponsored the event from 2015?

16. In which season did Ronnie O'Sullivan win the Masters and the Champion of Champions, despite being ranked 19th in the world?

17. The term 'Triple Crown' refers to winning the three most prestigious tournaments in Snooker. Which three tournaments?

18. In which year was the UK Championship Final first contested by two overseas players, Neil Robertson and Liang Wenbo?

19. Alongside Steve Davis, which other player has won the World Snooker Championship six times, one title behind the record of seven set by Stephen Hendry?

20. Following changes to the format in 1997, how many frames are the World Championship Semi-Finals played over?

TENNIS

1. Who has won the most Women's Wimbledon Singles Titles in the Open Era?

2. How many French Open Titles has Rafael Nadal won?

3. Who did Andy Murray defeat in the 2016 Wimbledon Final to become first Englishman to win multiple Wimbledon Single titles since Fred Perry in 1936?

4. Which player became the first British woman to win a WTA singles title since 1988, after her victory at the Japan Open in 2012?

5. Which was the first Grand Slam Singles title that Novak Djokovic won?

6. In which year did Roger Federer turn professional?

7. Which women's player won all four Grand Slams in 1988?

8. Name the two other players to have won a French Open title during the 2010s, alongside Rafael Nadal's dominance of eight titles during the decade?

9. What nationality in 2019 Women's Wimbledon Champion, Simona Halep?

10. Which player defeated Kei Nishikori to win the 2014 US Open, and then reach the 2017 Wimbledon and 2018 Australian Open Finals, losing to Roger Federer on both occasions?

11. In which year did the ATP World Tour Finals move to London?

12. In 2010, Rafael Nadal won 3 out of 4 Grand Slams. Which Grand Slam did he fail to win?

13. Who are the most successful Tennis Doubles pair in the Open Era?

14. In which year was the first Wimbledon Championships held?

15. Which Grand Slam Tournament is played first in the calendar year?

16. Which two players reached the Men's Wimbledon Final in three consecutive years: 1988, 1989, and 1990?

17. Who is the last player to win consecutive Women's singles Grand Slam titles, after she followed her US Open victory by winning the Australian Open the following year?

18. In which year did the Open Era begin, and who were the first winners of Wimbledon for Men and Women in the Open Era?

19. Which country won back-to-back Davis Cup titles in 2012 and 2013, defeating Spain and Serbia respectively in the finals?

20. Which Men's Player was the first to complete the Career Golden Grand Slam – winning the four Grand Slams and the Olympic Gold Medal in Singles?

TOP 10s

Using your sporting knowledge, can you fill in the answers for the following Top 10 lists?

QUESTION ONE

Name the Top Ten Countries for Gold Medals at all Summer Olympics since 2000 combined.

1		241
2		211
3		122
4		117
5		80
6		80
7		76
8		62
9		58
10		57

QUESTION TWO

Name the Top Ten most capped England Men's Cricket ODI
Players since 2010.

1		*210*
2		*158*
3		*157*
4		*121*
5		*113*
6		*107*
7		*106*
8		*105*
9		*95*
10		*82*

QUESTION THREE

Name the Top Ten English Premier League football Clubs by combined points from the 2010/11 season until, and including, the 2018/19 season.

1		745
2		664
3		644
4		640
5		625
6		594
7		503
8		367
9		366
10		365

QUESTION FOUR

Name the last Ten Sport Stars to win BBC Sports Personality of the Year Award.

1		*2021*
2		*2020*
3		*2019*
4		*2018*
5		*2017*
6		*2016, 2015, 2013*
7		*2014*
8		*2012*
9		*2011*
10		*2010*

QUESTION FIVE

Name the Top Ten Run Scorers in the Ashes since 1990.

1	(Aus) - 3044
2	(Eng) – 2493
3	(Aus) – 2476
4	(Aus) – 2357
5	(Aus) – 2241
6	(Aus) – 2204
7	(Eng) – 2158
8	(Eng) – 2016
9	(Eng) – 1983
10	(Aus) - 1888

QUESTION SIX

Name the Top Ten Premier League Assist Makers.

1		162
2		111
3		103
4		102
5		96
6		94
7		93
8		92
9		81
10		80

QUESTION SEVEN

Name the Top Ten most capped England Rugby Union Players.

1		*115*
2		*114*
3		*97*
4		*95*
5		*91*
6		*91*
7		*85*
8		*85*
9		*84*
10		*84*

QUESTION EIGHT

Name the Top Ten Wicket Takers in the Ashes since 1990.

1	(Aus) - 195
2	(Aus) – 157
3	(Eng) – 131
4	(Eng) – 112
5	(Aus) – 101
6	(Aus) – 87
7	(Aus) – 80
8	(Eng) – 74
9	(Aus) – 74
10	(Aus) - 73

QUESTION NINE

Name the Top Ten Premier League Players ordered by Appearances.

1		*653*
2		*632*
3		*609*
4		*589*
5		*572*
6		*535*
7		*516*
8		*514*
9		*508*
10		*505*

QUESTION TEN

Name the Top Ten Men's Tennis Players with the most Grand Slam Tournament Titles.

1		22
2		21
3		20
4		14
5		12
6		11
7		11
8		10
9		8
10		8

QUESTION ELEVEN

Name the Top Ten Women's Tennis Players with the most Grand Slam Tournament Titles.

1		23
2		22
3		18
4		18
5		11
6		9
7		8
8		7
9		7
10		7

QUESTION TWELVE

Name the Top Ten Countries ranked by number of matches won at FIFA World Cups, up until, and including, the 2018 World Cup.

1		73
2		67
3		45
4		43
5		34
6		30
7		29
8		27
9		24
10		19

QUESTION THIRTEEN

Name the Top Ten Cricket Counties ordered by number of County Championships won – if two counties share the same number of titles, ordered by most recent title.

1		33
2		20
3		13
4		9
5		8
6		8
7		7
8		6
9		5
10		3

QUESTION FOURTEEN

Name the Top Ten Formula One Drivers with the Most
Championship Titles.

1		7
2		7
3		5
4		4
5		4
6		3
7		3
8		3
9		3
10		3

QUESTION FIFTEEN

Name the Top Ten Most Decorated Great British Olympic Athletes
– by total medals won.

1	*9 (7 x G, 2 x S)*
2	*8 (5 x G, 1 x S, 2 x B)*
3	*7 (6 x G, 1 x S)*
4	*6 (5 x G, 1 x S)*
5	*6 (5 x G, 1 x B)*
6	*6 (3 x G, 1 x S, 2 x B)*
7	*6 (3 x G, 3 x B)*
8	*6 (1 x G, 5 x S)*
9	*5 (4 x G, 1 x S)*
10	*5 (3 x G, 2 x S)*

QUESTION SIXTEEN

Name the Top Ten Most UEFA Champions League/European Cup Trophies – if teams are tied on number of titles, ordered by most recent.

1		14
2		7
3		6
4		6
5		5
6		4
7		3
8		3
9		2
10		2

QUESTION SEVENTEEN

Name the Top Ten Football Clubs to have won the most England Top Division League Titles.

1		20
2		19
3		13
4		9
5		8
6		7
7		6
8		6
9		4
10		4

QUESTION EIGHTEEN

Name the Top Ten Sports ordered by number of Olympic Gold Medals won by Team Great Britain.

1		55 Golds
2		38 Golds
3		31 Golds
4		31 Golds
5		20 Golds
6		20 Golds
7		17 Golds
8		13 Golds
9		13 Golds
10		5 Golds

QUESTION NINETEEN

Name the Top Ten Largest UK Stadiums by Capacity.

1		90,000
2		82,000
3		74,140
4		73,971
5		67,144
6		62,850
7		62,500
8		60,411
9		60,260
10		55,097

QUESTION TWENTY

Name the Top Ten most Wins at the Golf Masters Tournament – if players are tied on titles, ordered by most recent.

1		6
2		5
3		4
4		3
5		3
6		3
7		3
8		3
9		2
10		2

WORDSEARCHES

Answers are provided for *Easy* wordsearches –
just find them within the grid. However, more
thought is required for *Hard* wordsearches...

EASY: Formula One Racing Teams

Try find these following 10 Formula One Teams in the Wordsearch below...

O	E	M	O	R	A	H	P	L	A	M	M	O	L	P
U	T	R	C	R	E	N	K	P	N	I	M	D	I	O
F	E	U	B	S	M	N	A	T	L	O	P	A	D	C
F	M	H	S	M	A	I	L	L	I	W	H	I	L	E
R	S	A	A	H	M	C	L	U	S	M	N	F	I	I
A	S	E	E	R	B	I	M	A	K	P	S	F	T	R
B	U	L	D	F	R	A	N	N	C	S	A	V	O	U
M	C	L	E	E	R	N	M	E	E	R	T	S	H	A
I	O	L	S	M	C	L	A	R	E	N	P	E	S	T
U	I	U	B	N	M	R	A	S	C	I	H	N	G	A
I	O	B	N	T	E	B	E	S	C	B	O	U	T	H
N	B	D	H	K	O	L	P	M	U	E	D	S	B	P
S	U	E	B	N	A	S	U	A	I	N	M	L	S	L
U	I	R	A	C	I	N	G	P	O	I	N	T	D	A
I	D	B	U	A	N	M	E	O	L	D	C	B	W	R

1. MERCEDES	6. RENAULT
2. HAAS	7. FERRARI
3. MCLAREN	8. ALPHA TAURI
4. ALFA ROMEO	9. WILLIAMS
5. RED BULL	10. RACING POINT

EASY: Netball Super League Teams

Try find these following 10 Netball Super League Teams...

E	D	Y	L	C	H	T	A	R	T	S	B	I	S	E
H	L	P	O	E	D	N	M	S	C	A	J	K	I	H
B	U	M	A	L	W	L	O	D	N	I	N	S	C	G
U	K	R	L	T	I	S	S	S	X	N	K	A	I	U
U	E	E	A	I	U	E	P	U	E	W	O	U	Y	O
S	H	T	G	C	T	S	W	R	W	G	T	E	E	R
T	I	S	A	R	A	C	E	N	S	S	S	G	W	O
U	D	E	O	W	A	S	Y	U	U	U	W	G	E	B
W	A	H	T	R	D	S	R	R	E	H	E	I	T	H
I	L	C	W	E	G	R	Y	T	Q	O	T	H	G	G
C	R	N	D	W	E	S	R	O	V	R	A	A	V	U
N	S	A	H	Y	R	R	U	P	W	Q	O	P	B	O
A	T	M	I	T	W	T	A	E	G	X	R	W	H	L
G	E	D	N	W	R	W	F	A	L	G	G	F	O	U
J	W	D	N	O	D	N	O	L	O	V	B	C	R	R

1. MANCHESTER	6. LOUGHBOROUGH
2. BATH	7. WASPS
3. LONDON	8. SURREY
4. SARACENS	9. SEVERN
5. STRATHCLYDE	10. CELTIC

EASY: Golf Terms

Try find these following 12 Golf Terms in the Wordsearch below...

A	E	C	V	T	Y	R	T	W	Y	H	N	L	I	Q
R	G	X	D	E	R	E	W	I	H	E	R	A	P	D
Y	S	D	G	E	H	R	F	R	A	U	G	K	E	R
W	G	O	H	N	U	E	H	A	H	T	W	S	H	O
T	B	H	I	U	E	T	E	Y	F	S	H	E	J	K
H	H	I	E	Y	C	T	G	A	J	O	J	N	W	R
N	W	T	R	B	D	U	S	W	R	E	L	G	A	E
E	B	P	Y	D	A	P	V	R	J	I	W	V	U	K
D	U	O	E	C	I	L	H	I	E	J	J	C	E	N
N	E	T	Q	H	U	E	E	A	H	V	M	G	B	U
E	O	E	C	X	W	I	H	F	E	S	I	P	M	B
E	P	Y	S	H	T	K	J	R	Q	W	L	R	L	B
R	Y	C	A	D	D	Y	E	U	G	R	B	W	D	F
G	E	U	Y	L	E	Y	V	K	J	R	N	I	S	W
S	B	N	E	P	D	N	E	E	T	J	W	A	G	J

1. BIRDIE	7. EAGLE
2. BOGEY	8. FAIRWAY
3. BUKER	9. GREEN
4. CADDY	10. PAR
5. CHIP	11. PUTTER
6. DRIVER	12. TEE

EASY: Premier League Top Scorers

Try find the following 10 Premier League Top Scorers...

E	N	M	O	W	E	N	G	C	N	N	F	B	N	E
E	D	B	P	D	A	U	S	D	R	A	P	M	A	L
O	O	S	O	V	E	T	R	H	F	B	L	S	H	L
F	I	R	E	R	A	E	H	S	W	S	M	H	D	O
E	H	K	P	N	O	R	R	T	G	F	U	E	C	Y
D	E	G	J	R	F	O	L	O	C	B	Y	G	U	H
B	U	O	T	A	H	E	N	R	Y	W	R	W	M	E
G	A	L	K	F	S	O	T	E	H	G	J	F	N	G
E	L	V	H	N	R	E	J	P	Y	N	B	B	G	O
B	S	X	T	H	F	G	T	A	G	W	S	S	R	R
M	P	E	S	E	O	N	E	G	E	F	V	H	Q	E
Y	M	L	D	T	I	S	J	W	I	N	E	K	T	U
D	S	O	W	H	R	E	L	W	O	F	A	F	F	G
S	F	C	R	G	I	L	F	J	U	J	K	N	I	A
G	L	Y	I	D	E	A	N	K	D	T	A	F	K	O

1. SHEARER	6. LAMPARD
2. ROONEY	7. HENRY
3. COLE	8. FOWLER
4. AGUERO	9. DEFOE
5. KANE	10. OWEN

EASY: International Rugby Union Nations

Find these Top 10 International Rugby Union teams based on Men's World Rugby Rankings...

N	D	A	J	N	L	S	I	H	U	J	N	H	F	H
R	S	C	O	T	L	A	N	D	F	R	N	C	A	I
J	G	H	B	F	S	J	I	K	U	G	N	C	B	A
N	M	S	R	E	D	N	A	L	E	R	I	O	P	N
L	E	R	V	H	N	J	F	S	E	R	T	U	B	I
G	J	U	A	H	G	B	M	K	F	L	S	Y	G	T
W	G	H	I	E	N	G	L	A	N	D	D	E	Z	N
A	V	S	L	A	Y	T	H	H	J	N	X	C	I	E
L	F	L	A	D	G	T	U	T	L	G	J	N	F	G
E	H	F	R	F	U	R	H	E	I	E	K	A	H	R
S	J	A	T	O	H	W	D	D	N	H	O	R	A	A
V	S	E	S	U	S	S	D	K	O	A	R	F	D	B
E	F	T	U	Y	V	H	V	I	D	R	P	A	D	V
Y	B	H	A	T	S	N	S	J	A	G	L	A	J	H
I	D	N	A	L	A	E	Z	W	E	N	D	D	J	O

1. IRELAND
2. FRANCE
3. SOUTH AFRICA
4. ENGLAND
5. NEW ZEALAND

6. AUSTRALIA
7. SCOTLAND
8. WALES
9. ARGENTINA
10. JAPAN

EASY: GB Women's Hockey Starting Lineup Gold Medal Match 2016 Olympics

Find the starting XI Surnames in the Gold Medal winning match for the GB Women Hockey vs Netherlands at Rio 2016...

R	W	B	B	E	W	H	D	N	E	S	N	W	O	T
I	F	N	J	B	M	T	A	F	D	G	L	V	H	E
C	J	E	E	S	F	E	N	H	H	G	G	A	E	T
H	F	T	N	L	W	R	S	N	K	J	R	M	S	J
A	E	J	D	R	L	U	O	T	M	R	F	M	V	N
R	B	H	B	J	V	U	N	H	R	E	B	Y	B	G
D	M	W	D	E	A	L	C	E	W	E	N	T	H	W
S	F	R	T	T	R	N	A	T	F	R	S	E	T	F
O	E	S	N	I	I	B	G	K	H	K	G	G	R	R
N	B	D	Y	H	T	F	J	Y	A	R	B	N	O	B
W	B	V	K	W	J	W	T	E	J	N	M	D	W	F
A	E	F	L	G	U	R	E	L	E	G	T	T	S	E
L	F	E	R	W	O	O	G	S	W	E	G	Y	N	Y
S	H	R	W	R	R	L	J	N	G	Y	S	O	U	K
H	N	M	D	O	E	L	C	A	M	O	G	L	F	J

1. *Maddie* HINCH
2. *Laura* UNSWORTH
3. *Crista* Cullen
4. *Hannah* MACLEOD
5. *Susannah* TOWNSEND
6. *Kate* RICHARDSON-WALSH
7. *Alex* DANSON
8. *Giselle* ANSLEY
9. *Sophie* BRAY
10. *Hollie* WEBB
11. *Nicola* WHITE

EASY: World Championship Snooker Winners

Find these 10 World Snooker Championship Winners...

R	E	B	D	O	N	M	W	G	K	V	O	S	A	I
W	T	Y	I	G	L	M	A	H	G	N	I	B	G	K
F	Y	R	E	K	O	J	P	D	T	E	R	D	R	N
S	N	I	G	G	I	H	R	G	R	C	H	J	H	O
H	H	K	W	L	W	S	H	L	W	E	J	T	J	S
R	S	J	R	P	F	R	H	J	B	L	K	K	T	T
N	F	T	H	J	M	P	K	G	T	T	O	D	G	R
A	V	A	E	M	R	U	R	E	P	N	P	H	E	E
V	U	Y	B	G	Y	O	R	S	T	F	R	T	E	B
I	Y	B	H	W	J	Y	W	T	S	K	D	D	H	O
L	B	D	K	P	G	H	F	I	B	U	H	N	S	R
L	L	I	U	T	R	T	J	U	J	T	D	R	J	H
U	E	U	R	R	D	U	M	T	F	E	H	O	K	T
S	S	T	B	Y	D	S	M	A	I	L	L	I	W	E
O	A	Y	K	O	V	J	L	O	L	E	J	L	K	S

1. *Judd* TRUMP
2. *Mark* WILLIAMS
3. *Mark* SELBY
4. *Stuart* BINGHAM
5. *Ronnie* O'SULLIVAN

6. *John* HIGGINS
7. *Neil* ROBERTSON
8. *Graeme* DOTT
9. *Shaun* MURPHY
10. *Peter* EBDON

EASY: Tennis Terms

Try find the following 10 Tennis Terms...

G	E	H	S	J	U	E	K	H	J	E	R	K	I	J
R	Y	D	R	D	M	A	L	S	D	N	A	R	G	E
T	L	J	K	A	P	T	J	S	E	U	L	E	Y	T
W	K	M	T	K	I	H	D	H	H	R	K	H	T	G
B	J	C	Y	D	R	J	F	R	E	T	V	K	E	H
G	H	R	R	H	E	K	K	K	U	E	T	E	J	S
S	E	Y	I	N	U	G	H	R	K	H	P	R	Y	C
T	T	K	Y	L	L	R	W	H	K	J	R	T	T	G
E	Y	F	K	O	L	Y	R	F	A	S	K	H	A	N
H	L	B	H	P	H	A	Y	E	E	H	S	E	T	M
L	K	D	E	L	J	Y	B	U	R	E	J	K	R	Y
G	Y	S	R	R	Y	E	H	J	B	R	Y	E	U	R
D	R	H	U	T	R	H	T	E	E	J	A	G	O	F
B	E	C	U	E	D	K	O	H	I	E	S	P	C	J
J	I	H	J	N	E	F	L	J	T	H	I	E	H	O

1. BALL		6. NET
2. COURT		7. SERVE
3. DEUCE		8. SET
4. GRAND SLAM		9. TIE BREAK
5. MATCH		10. UMPIRE

EASY: Rugby Union Stadiums

Find the following 10 Rugby Union Stadiums...

Y	H	J	T	W	I	C	K	E	N	H	A	M	N	J
E	M	O	R	D	O	L	E	V	E	D	A	T	S	D
C	U	B	J	B	H	F	R	T	S	J	G	J	O	S
N	M	U	R	R	A	Y	F	I	E	L	D	M	J	O
A	U	J	U	G	B	N	M	S	V	E	R	O	P	L
R	I	A	H	Y	M	I	L	L	E	N	I	U	M	D
F	D	M	H	C	U	U	I	L	H	Y	B	F	R	I
E	A	I	G	T	H	U	I	D	G	T	R	B	H	E
D	T	L	O	H	T	F	E	D	N	G	R	D	G	R
E	S	G	E	L	L	I	S	P	A	R	K	I	U	F
D	B	S	I	Y	I	H	F	R	C	T	L	O	D	I
A	N	W	E	O	T	P	W	H	G	Y	S	P	I	E
T	F	Y	T	C	H	N	M	K	I	Y	G	Z	D	L
S	U	E	H	Y	I	H	N	E	R	S	L	O	N	D
O	C	I	P	M	I	L	O	O	I	D	A	T	S	A

1. FNB STADIUM (*South Africa*)
2. ANZ STADIUM (*Australia*)
3. TWICKENHAM (*England*)
4. STADE DE FRANCE (*France*)
5. MILLENIUM *Stadium* (*Wales*)
6. STADIO OLIMPICO (*Italy*)
7. MURRAYFIELD *Stadium* (*Scotla*
8. ELLIS PARK *Stadium* (*South Afri*
9. SOLDIER FIELD (*United States*)
10. STADE VELODROME (*France*)

EASY: Artistic Gymnastic Disciplines

Try find the following 8 Gymnastic Disciplines in the Wordsearch...

Y	H	Y	B	R	A	J	U	N	U	O	K	H	Y	G
Y	N	G	R	M	A	E	B	E	C	N	A	L	A	B
E	R	S	D	F	N	M	K	I	U	D	E	R	T	U
S	B	G	U	I	M	H	G	R	D	G	T	S	S	O
R	L	N	J	Y	G	F	T	Y	U	G	P	R	J	H
O	D	I	R	H	I	B	J	U	N	A	A	O	P	I
H	O	R	I	Z	O	N	T	A	L	B	A	R	R	F
L	W	L	T	N	B	R	O	O	L	F	C	L	Y	U
E	U	L	O	R	G	T	A	E	B	J	G	L	I	Y
M	R	I	W	O	S	J	L	S	U	F	W	O	T	T
M	E	T	E	B	X	L	G	U	E	A	R	D	E	E
O	V	S	T	A	A	F	W	H	A	R	T	G	B	T
P	H	Y	J	R	T	O	R	M	I	V	O	S	J	I
R	J	A	A	S	J	L	P	R	K	H	K	B	H	K
O	P	P	S	R	A	B	N	E	V	E	N	U	M	M

1. VAULT	5. POMMEL HORSE
2. UNEVEN BARS	6. STILL RINGS
3. BALANCE BEAM	7. PARALLEL BARS
4. FLOOR	8. HORIZONTAL BAR

EASY: Golf Masters Winners

Find the 10 winners of the Masters Tournament...

S	C	O	T	T	M	N	M	M	S	R	M	F	H	X
H	G	A	A	A	I	C	R	A	G	U	G	N	E	E
F	S	G	C	H	F	V	G	N	V	K	R	J	M	R
S	I	K	V	G	Q	G	E	G	H	J	V	A	G	G
E	H	F	D	A	G	D	S	F	D	H	T	D	N	G
T	G	R	E	L	F	F	E	H	C	S	M	F	M	M
G	F	L	E	M	D	J	V	E	U	C	F	Y	F	W
J	S	R	R	J	E	H	M	Y	G	G	E	K	H	I
D	A	D	B	T	H	F	A	G	J	Y	X	T	D	L
S	N	G	M	D	F	M	K	D	B	J	E	H	B	L
V	O	K	H	F	A	R	S	M	D	I	B	V	M	E
N	S	M	F	G	S	D	R	N	P	E	M	D	H	T
J	T	H	E	J	O	H	N	S	O	N	K	W	L	T
D	A	T	S	O	N	Y	D	F	J	R	U	R	G	B
W	W	E	W	K	G	L	S	H	G	F	F	H	E	V

1. *Scottie* SCHEFFLER	6. *Sergio* GARCIA
2. *Hideki* MATSUYAMA	7. *Danny* WILLETT
3. *Dustin* JOHNSON	8. *Jordan* SPIETH
4. *Tiger* WOODS	9. *Bubba* WATSON
5. *Patrick* REED	10. *Adam* SCOTT

EASY: Rugby Positions

Try find the following 10 Rugby Union positions...

S	S	F	T	A	A	W	O	R	D	N	O	C	E	S
D	F	H	I	S	W	O	F	S	T	O	A	H	Y	A
G	L	L	K	F	R	U	L	F	J	T	W	Y	R	S
Y	Y	L	A	G	F	U	A	G	J	R	D	R	U	F
Y	H	O	J	N	S	R	H	H	N	B	S	E	H	T
E	A	Y	B	U	K	E	M	J	T	R	V	H	W	H
T	L	R	G	T	W	E	U	K	R	G	F	I	W	G
Y	F	B	W	E	C	R	R	J	E	D	N	O	E	I
J	E	H	E	G	G	T	C	Y	A	G	D	U	T	E
K	T	E	B	H	G	N	S	R	E	S	A	T	G	R
N	P	W	E	K	E	E	R	R	E	K	O	O	H	E
D	O	G	T	L	T	C	T	T	Y	V	D	L	E	B
D	R	H	O	L	I	A	U	E	I	D	D	P	E	M
W	P	J	L	L	P	C	J	W	L	W	I	E	T	U
F	H	K	K	C	A	B	L	L	U	F	P	F	I	N

1. PROP
2. HOOKER
3. SECOND ROW
4. FLANKER
5. NUMBER EIGHT

6. SCRUM HALF
7. FLY HALF
8. WINGER
9. CENTRE
10. FULL BACK

EASY: 1966 FIFA World Cup England Starting XI

Find the Surnames of the England 1966 World Cup Final Starting XI...

S	R	E	T	E	P	Y	T	O	T	I	L	I	O	I
T	O	S	C	J	O	E	R	S	E	L	I	T	S	S
R	T	V	B	U	L	S	Y	L	A	W	E	E	S	D
W	E	H	N	T	N	A	R	B	R	E	T	R	F	F
G	G	Y	G	E	R	O	O	M	E	R	T	T	M	B
U	S	R	H	S	E	V	Y	H	D	H	U	H	H	G
I	S	O	E	V	D	Z	O	F	U	U	W	N	T	R
N	C	W	S	V	S	C	L	R	O	T	S	V	R	E
D	H	U	N	T	C	S	S	P	L	E	G	S	E	G
E	A	S	G	Z	W	T	B	C	W	G	Y	V	T	J
S	R	V	R	D	T	V	E	W	I	D	O	G	H	J
A	L	N	T	E	E	C	E	E	L	S	P	J	E	N
F	T	J	O	A	T	W	T	R	S	K	N	A	B	F
H	O	L	P	M	O	R	U	G	O	J	I	L	S	E
J	N	C	H	A	R	L	T	O	N	G	K	O	P	S

1. *Gordan* BANKS *(GK)*
2. *George* COHEN *(DEF)*
3. *Jack* CHARLTON *(DEF)*
4. *Bobby* MOORE *(DEF)*
5. *Ray* WILSON *(DEF)*
6. *Nobby* STILES *(MID)*
7. *Alan* BALL *(MID)*
8. *Bobby* CHARLTON *(MID)*
9. *Martin* PETERS *(MID)*
10. *Geoff* HURST *(ST)*
11. *Roger* HUNT *(ST)*

HARD: Football Grounds

*Try find the following **Stadium Names** of the following 10 Football Clubs...*

C	V	I	C	A	R	A	G	E	R	O	A	D	R	V
O	I	S	G	N	D	G	S	H	F	E	F	D	C	V
L	L	K	D	E	A	W	E	C	E	N	T	D	L	O
D	O	R	T	F	U	T	T	S	M	A	R	D	D	Y
T	D	A	I	U	E	A	A	F	E	L	N	F	W	D
R	C	P	D	I	R	V	R	O	R	L	G	E	Y	A
A	S	T	K	H	I	F	I	L	C	L	W	T	O	O
F	R	S	Z	R	A	F	M	D	W	A	U	H	U	R
F	R	R	Q	U	A	O	E	O	D	M	P	L	C	W
O	A	U	W	E	L	P	F	P	O	A	U	V	A	O
R	X	H	A	I	T	H	A	S	V	R	P	O	D	R
D	C	L	N	Y	I	P	F	L	Y	B	A	L	O	R
L	N	E	P	S	R	K	F	D	L	E	I	F	N	A
K	U	S	T	R	A	U	K	M	L	I	C	I	L	C
X	U	D	E	X	B	N	L	C	A	R	V	N	I	K

1. ARSENAL
2. ASTON VILLA
3. BURNLEY
4. CRYSTAL PALACE
5. LIVERPOOL
6. MANCHESTER UNITED
7. NORWICH CITY
8. SHEFFIELD UNITED
9. WATFORD
10. WOLVES

HARD: England's 2019 Cricket World Cup Final Starting XI

Find the Surnames of England's 2019 Cricket World Cup Final Starting XI (hint: First names provided) ...

T	O	L	I	P	L	U	N	K	E	T	T	I	N	C
D	A	T	B	E	R	W	S	S	U	C	M	K	Y	L
T	P	N	T	M	E	A	R	O	M	W	O	Z	C	R
R	K	R	Y	Y	H	E	R	N	P	B	T	O	R	D
E	C	W	M	O	C	B	E	A	C	O	R	T	P	L
T	W	O	M	B	R	R	J	G	O	J	A	S	I	N
L	P	T	R	A	A	L	S	R	E	G	I	D	H	M
E	N	S	R	D	T	W	O	O	N	C	I	L	P	U
B	T	R	E	W	T	I	Y	M	T	H	S	G	L	S
A	X	I	V	K	B	M	L	N	S	T	O	M	M	R
O	U	A	W	N	A	M	S	A	G	E	P	E	T	F
Y	J	B	F	G	R	O	R	I	O	F	K	O	D	E
E	G	R	A	S	O	A	W	Y	R	S	W	O	W	P
S	W	S	E	G	T	S	I	R	T	L	O	G	T	I
C	R	E	L	T	T	U	B	Y	G	W	I	N	K	S

1. *Jason*	7. *Chris*
2. *Jonathan*	8. *Liam*
3. *Joe*	9. *Jofra*
4. *Eoin*	10. *Adil*
5. *Ben*	11. *Mark*
6. *Jos*	

HARD: Heptathlon Events

Find the seven events in a Heptathlon in the Wordsearch below...

2	0	L	R	U	M	T	U	P	T	O	H	S	6	J
1	P	S	O	M	L	S	H	5	Y	M	E	P	O	M
N	S	A	Y	N	7	C	B	9	A	L	P	J	P	K
W	R	V	H	I	G	L	O	E	D	1	2	7	N	8
8	H	G	O	N	L	J	W	R	O	S	I	3	O	0
5	C	M	N	D	7	B	U	9	L	I	W	V	N	0
H	J	K	4	6	P	H	1	M	L	O	M	S	8	M
N	P	M	E	T	M	R	U	B	P	6	1	0	J	R
R	I	3	L	0	M	8	H	R	U	D	L	O	7	U
U	7	L	0	P	Y	B	F	K	B	7	V	M	C	N
E	G	1	E	W	F	2	0	0	M	R	U	N	I	L
G	K	5	P	V	5	N	F	4	M	7	D	1	0	P
B	M	7	L	S	A	6	J	U	A	V	L	I	N	W
K	C	0	P	M	U	J	H	G	I	H	P	L	S	N
4	W	D	J	3	J	6	I	A	V	E	L	S	J	A

1.

2.

3.

4.

5.

6.

7.

HARD: American Football Team Names

Complete the following NFL Team names and find the Nickname in the wordsearch below...

E	S	A	S	E	I	E	N	L	W	T	O	B	E	A
A	E	R	C	U	N	Y	U	K	E	I	R	K	Y	H
S	A	U	H	C	O	W	B	O	Y	S	W	S	W	O
B	H	B	U	V	S	K	W	A	T	H	J	D	S	I
E	A	M	E	E	S	S	A	F	Y	S	F	H	C	H
Y	W	W	L	I	N	T	C	M	L	T	R	B	B	T
S	K	G	S	Y	I	N	V	A	U	O	G	A	X	R
T	S	N	N	O	K	A	N	J	D	I	W	H	E	A
E	V	S	O	T	S	I	B	N	A	R	S	V	M	B
E	O	O	C	N	D	G	R	H	F	T	B	K	R	T
L	J	C	L	R	E	A	T	F	N	A	J	W	U	U
E	A	T	A	Z	R	D	A	R	D	P	E	V	G	W
R	R	C	F	W	A	N	U	E	W	R	D	Y	K	I
S	U	D	W	Y	R	U	N	T	A	I	H	O	H	P
A	T	S	E	L	G	A	E	O	J	K	J	L	F	L

1. Arizona	6.	New York
2. Atlanta	7.	Philadelphia
3. Chicago	8.	Pittsburgh
4. Dallas	9.	Seattle
5. New England	10.	Washington

HARD: Previous 10 England Football Team Managers

*Find the Surnames of the last 10 England Football Managers
(hint: First names provided) ...*

N	N	V	M	E	N	L	N	E	R	A	L	C	C	M
O	M	W	M	E	A	O	H	O	J	D	K	I	M	Y
S	V	D	K	G	G	I	E	L	B	G	P	W	J	F
S	A	S	H	D	E	C	R	A	E	P	J	H	T	S
K	R	I	O	B	E	U	I	K	E	S	V	S	D	F
I	I	T	S	U	K	H	K	G	V	G	W	H	M	N
R	R	E	D	J	T	A	Y	L	O	R	R	M	G	O
E	J	R	B	E	S	H	L	M	P	J	O	S	S	S
R	B	G	E	B	O	P	G	R	L	K	I	T	J	N
T	A	D	I	D	C	F	C	A	P	E	L	L	O	I
U	R	V	G	I	W	V	K	E	T	O	U	K	J	K
S	L	S	Y	O	H	C	W	C	D	E	Y	S	Y	L
D	O	N	O	E	B	N	E	B	T	M	T	T	R	I
N	T	K	L	H	A	M	S	J	L	R	E	J	S	W
A	G	A	L	L	A	R	D	Y	C	E	A	K	J	T

1. *Gareth*	6. *Steve*
2. *Sam*	7. *Sven-Göran*
3. *Roy*	8. *Peter*
4. *Stuart*	9. *Kevin*
5. *Fabio*	10. *Howard*

HARD: IPL Cricket Teams

Find the Eight Cities that are home to these IPL Teams
(hint: Franchise name is provided)...

A	H	J	I	O	N	F	R	D	B	H	J	U	V	B
I	A	B	M	U	M	S	B	K	X	C	K	D	B	N
J	M	F	H	G	A	Y	N	J	P	O	L	A	S	U
N	I	N	S	D	I	M	K	O	J	X	C	B	O	P
A	N	H	F	I	G	M	G	J	G	F	R	A	S	B
H	L	O	B	J	C	P	J	B	S	B	S	R	A	A
T	N	G	N	J	B	H	J	A	I	B	J	E	J	T
S	S	V	B	H	F	Y	E	J	A	U	N	D	K	A
A	U	N	I	S	J	M	J	N	S	S	J	Y	S	K
J	J	U	H	X	B	C	D	U	N	S	U	H	N	L
A	C	H	L	E	N	N	J	P	S	A	B	K	O	O
R	I	B	E	S	Y	B	J	G	D	F	I	S	K	K
P	O	B	D	S	B	J	U	G	E	D	V	H	U	K
L	O	G	G	S	B	N	H	S	T	R	N	K	M	L
O	E	R	O	L	A	G	N	A	B	C	T	Y	N	S

1. *Super Kings*
2. *Capitals*
3. *Kings*
4. *Knight Riders*

5. *Indians*
6. *Royals*
7. *Royal Challengers*
8. *Sunrisers*

HARD: Summer and Winter Olympic Host Cities

Find the 10 host cities of the Summer and Winter Olympics between 2000-2018 (hint: Country provided) ...

T	Y	V	Y	T	I	C	E	K	A	L	T	L	A	S
N	H	Y	E	R	V	S	H	N	O	D	N	O	L	S
G	H	S	Y	D	N	E	Y	L	A	H	R	K	P	E
O	J	S	J	I	A	S	E	O	Y	T	E	J	O	T
R	E	F	N	G	G	F	S	T	R	E	D	F	L	E
I	R	C	D	O	N	G	H	F	E	W	G	B	F	F
E	T	E	R	T	I	A	N	D	S	I	H	D	B	E
N	U	T	E	L	J	B	H	V	H	G	E	E	D	R
A	K	I	V	D	I	D	D	C	B	H	R	D	E	D
J	F	J	U	S	E	E	O	N	G	J	U	A	W	B
E	E	G	O	W	B	S	F	H	T	N	O	T	F	R
D	G	E	C	F	E	H	R	D	R	I	O	H	B	T
O	N	T	N	G	R	T	T	O	E	R	R	E	B	U
I	M	I	A	J	Y	J	I	J	W	U	E	N	Y	O
R	D	J	V	K	H	M	K	P	L	T	S	S	N	P

1. South Korea	6. China
2. Brazil	7. Italy
3. Russia	8. Greece
4. England	9. United States
5. Canada	10. Australia

ANSWERS

GUESS THE ATHLETE

1. Adam Peaty

2. Lewis Hamilton

3. Laura Kenny

4. Jessica Ennis-Hill

5. Anthony Joshua

6. Jamie Vardy

7. Stuart Broad

8. Lucy Bronze

9. Amy Williams

10. Rory McIlroy

11. Jonny Wilkinson

12. Gareth Southgate

13. Andy Farrell

14. Ian Botham

15. Beth Tweddle

16. Steve Davis

17. Sue Barker

18. Alex Ferguson

19. Elise Christie

20. Daley Thompson

21. Heather Knight

22. Mo Farah

23. Kyle Edmund

24. Jonathan Brownlee

25. Steven Gerrard

IF THESE ARE THE EVENTS, WHAT IS THE YEAR?

SPORTING EVENTS	WHAT YEAR DID THEY TAKE PLACE?
1. Manchester United become the first English side to complete the treble. 2. Lindsey Davenport won Women's Wimbledon Championship. 3. Michael Johnson sets new world-record in 400m in Seville (43.18s).	**1999**
1. Arsenal played their final game at Highbury on May 7th. 2. Italy won the FIFA World Cup; however, the final will be remembered for the actions of Zinedine Zidane. 3. Rafael Nadal wins his second French Open Title in as many years, with Roger Federer winning the other three Grand Slam Singles Titles.	**2006**
1. First Olympics to be held in South America.	

2. Leicester overcame 5000/1 odds to win the Premier League. 3. Denver Broncos won Super Bowl.	**2016**
1. Mike Weir becomes the first Canadian and the first left-handed golfer to win the Masters. 2. English Twenty20 Cup is first held, being the first professional T20 league in the world. 3. England win the Rugby Union World Cup, 20-17 after extra time.	**2003**
1. Two English sides competed in the UEFA Champions League Final, which ended in penalties. 2. Rajasthan Royals win the inaugural Indian Premier League. 3. USA win the Ryder Cup 16½ - 11½, to end the streak of three successive victories for Europe.	**2008**
1. Lizzie Yarnold won Great Britain's only Gold Medal	

at the Winter Olympics. 2. Germany defeated Argentina in the FIFA World Cup Final. 3. Nadal wins a record ninth French Open Title.	**2014**
1. Brazil won the FIFA World Cup, hosted in the USA. 2. Commonwealth Games held in British Columbia, Canada. 3. Brian Lara scored 375 runs in a single day vs England in April, before later breaking the record for the highest first-class score of 501* for Warwickshire.	**1994**
1. Australia wins the Rugby Union World Cup. 2. Michael Stich wins his first, and only, Wimbledon title. 3. Super Bowl XXV is won by the New York Giants 20-19 over the Buffalo Bills.	**1991**
1. Sir Ben Ainslie wins his first Olympic Gold Medal. 2. Los Angeles Lakers win	

their first NBA title in twelve years, defeating Indiana Pacers 4 games to 2. 3. Tiger Woods becomes the first golfer to win three majors in a calendar year since Ben Hogan in 1953.	**2000**
1. England win the ICC Cricket World Cup Final, defeating New Zealand in the final via a Super Over. 2. Tiger Woods returns to win the Masters – his 5th Green Jacket. 3. South Africa win the Rugby Union World Cup.	**2019**
1. Diego Forlan wins Golden Ball at the FIFA World Cup. 2. Graeme McDowell wins the US Open, ending a 40-year drought for Europeans at the tournament. 3. Winter Olympics held in Vancouver.	**2010**
1. Justin Gatlin wins his first	

Olympic Gold Medal, and in the same Games wins Silver in the 4 x 100m. 2. Best Mate wins the Cheltenham Gold Cup for the third consecutive time. 3. Arsenal completed the Invincible Season, completing the English Premier League without a single defeat.	**2004**
1. The Champions League took on its current name "UEFA Champions League", with Barcelona winning the competition. 2. England lose in the Cricket World Cup Final against Pakistan. 3. Summer Olympics held in Barcelona.	**1992**
1. Mike Tyson bites off a piece of Evander Holyfield's ear in the third round of their WBA Heavyweight title fight. 2. Tiger Woods wins his first Masters title. 3. Athletics World Championships are held	**1997**

at the Olympic Stadium, Athens.	
1. Brazil win their 5th FIFA World Cup, defeating Germany 2-0 in the final. 2. Peter Ebdon beats Stephen Hendry 18-17 in the World Snooker Championship Final. 3. Commonwealth games held in Manchester, with England finishing second in the medal table with 54 golds.	**2002**
1. Stuart Broad takes 8-15 to help dismiss Australia for 60 at Trent Bridge. 2. Jordan Spieth wins the Masters. 3. Great Britain wins the Davis Cup.	**2015**
1. Chelsea defeated Bayern Munich after penalties in the Champions League Final. 2. Great Britain finished 3rd in the Olympic Medal Table with 29 Gold medals.	**2012**

3. Europe achieved one of the greatest comebacks in Ryder Cup history by winning eight and tying one of the twelve singles matches, to win the cup 14½–13½.	
1. UEFA Champions League Final provided great entertainment, as Liverpool overcame a 3-goal deficit to win on penalties. 2. England won their first Ashes in 18 years, with Andrew Flintoff being named Man of the Series. 3. British and Irish Lions Tour to New Zealand suffered a 3-0 whitewash.	**2005**
1. Manchester City become the first Premier League side to reach 100 points in a season. 2. Alistair Cook scores a century vs India in his final Test Match. 3. England reach FIFA World Cup Semi Finals, losing after extra-time to	**2018**

Croatia.	
1. England completed a 3-1 Ashes win down under. 2. Leinster beat Northampton Saints in the Heineken Cup Final to win their second title in three years. 3. Manchester United won their 19th English League Title.	**2011**
1. Ronnie O'Sullivan wins his first World Snooker Championship. 2. Lleyton Hewitt wins his first Grand Slam Singles title, and in the same year becomes World Number One. 3. Cheltenham Gold Cup not held due to the foot-and-mouth crisis.	**2001**
1. Steffi Graff wins 3 out of 4 Grand Slams, failing to win the Australian Open, in which Monica Seles was victorious. 2. United States wins 101 Olympic Medals in	**1996**

Atlanta. 3. Dallas Cowboys won Super Bowl XXX 27-17 over the Pittsburgh Steelers.	
1. Peter "Snakebite" Wright wins his first PDC World Championship title, defeating Michael Van Gerwen in the final. 2. Tyson Fury wins his rematch versus Deontay Wilder. 3. The Summer Olympic Games is postponed for only its fourth time in modern Olympic Games history, the previous three times due to war.	**2020**
1. England regained the Ashes, winning the series 2-1. 2. Ireland completed their first RBS Six Nations Grand Slam. 3. FC Barcelona win the UEFA Champions League, beating Manchester United 2-0 in Rome.	**2009**

1. Buster Douglas defeated Mike Tyson to become the World's Unified Heavyweight Champion, in a huge upset. 2. Nick Faldo wins his second Masters tournament in as many years. 3. Stephen Hendry beat Jimmy White 18-12 in the World Snooker Championship Final.	**1990**
1. Phil Taylor won his first PDC World Championship. 2. Blackburn Rovers won their first Premier League title, denying Manchester United a hattrick of titles. 3. Pete Sampras won both Wimbledon and US Open Titles, both for the third time.	**1995**
1. Australia completes an Ashes Series 5-0 whitewash over England, and later the same year, win the Cricket World Cup. 2. Joe Calzaghe becomes	**2007**

the first undisputed super middleweight champion. 3. South Africa win the Rugby World Cup in France, defeating England 15-6 in the final.	
1. Grand National was won by One for Arthur at 14/1 odds. 2. Australia defeated England in the final of the Rugby League World Cup held in Australia, New Zealand, and Papua New Guinea. 3. Usain Bolt retires.	**2017**
1. Andy Murray wins his first Wimbledon title. 2. Justin Rose wins the US Open, winning his first major of his career. 3. Miami Heat won their third NBA Championship Title, having successfully defended their title from the year before.	**2013**
1. Michael Jordan won his final NBA Championship with the Chicago Bulls, in	

a season known as the "Last Dance". 2. France wins a home FIFA World Cup, defeating Brazil 3-0 in the final. 3. Great Britain wins one bronze medal at the Winter Olympics in Nagano, Japan.	**1998**
1. Manchester United win the inaugural Premier League Title, their first league title in 26 years. 2. Shane Warn bowls the 'Ball of the Century' to Mike Gatting in the first Ashes test at Old Trafford. 3. The Grand National was described as the 'Race that Never Was', as the rave was void following a series of incidents, including starting tape malfunctioning, false starts, and horses failing to stop.	**1993**

MATHS QUESTIONS

1. 75

    a. $((7 \times 5) + 40)$

2. 24

    a. $((30 + 6) - 12)$

3. 16

    a. $((40 + 36) - 60)$

4. 8

    a. $(3 + 5)$

5. 60

    a. (10×6)

6. 42

    a. (6×7)

7. 1,**978**

    a. $((2003 - 7) - 18)$

8. 59

    a. $((100 - 30) - 11)$

9. 81

    a. (((300 + 100) / 4) − 19)

10. 120

    a. ((((22 X 10) + 400) − 20) / 5)

11. 227

    a. ((170 + 7) + 50)

12. 500

    a. ((50 + 50) + 400)

13. 9

    a. (((7 + 38) − 9) / 4)

14. 360

    a. ((18 X 5) X 4)

15. 51

    a. ((26 X 3) − (2 + 3 + 4 + 5 + 6 + 7)

16. 260

    a. (((23 X 6) − 25) + 147)

17. 21

    a. ((20 + 14) − 13)

18. 108

    a. $((13 \times 10) - 22)$

19. 2,027

    a. $((2019 - 2) + 10)$

20. 32

    a. $((3 \times 9) + 5)$

QUESTIONS BY SPORT

AMERICAN FOOTBALL

1. Arizona Cardinals

2. 22nd October 1939

3. New England Patriots (11 appearances, winning 6)

4. Tom Brady (4 MVPs)

5. Jerry Rice (48 points)

6. 75 points. San Francisco 49ers 49 – 26 San Diego, January 1995

7. Vince Lombardi Trophy

8. Cleveland Browns, Detroit Lions, Jacksonville Jaguars, Houston Texans

9. Ken Norton Jr. (Dallas for Super Bowl 27 & Super Bowl 28, and 49ers in Super Bowl 29)

10. Chris Haley

11. Green Bay Packers

12. Tampa Bay Buccaneers

13. 1998, drafted by the Indianapolis Colts

14. Jerry Rice – 208

15. Tennessee Titans – lost to the Titans 3 times

16. Minnesota Vikings

17. Jason Hanson, Detroit Lions (1992 – 2012)

18. Sixteen

19. Bill Belichick, New England Patriots

20. Dallas Cowboys

ATHLETICS/ OLYMPICS

1. Jamaica, 2012 Olympics (36.84 seconds)

2. Sanya Richards-Ross (United States)

3. Jim Hines (USA), 1968 Mexico Olympics

4. United States: Brianna Rollins (Gold), Nia Ali (Silver), Kristi Castlin (Bronze)

5. Kelly Sotherton

6. 4th August 2012, GB won 6 medals

7. Men's: Finland (7 Golds); Women's: Ethiopia (5 Golds)

8. Silver

9. Louis Smith – Pommel Horse (Bronze in 2008; Silver in 2012, 2016)

10. Delhi (2010), Glasgow (2014), Gold Coast (2018)

11. Men's: Bradley Wiggins: 8 medals (5 x Gold, 1 x Silver, 2 x Bronze). Women's: Katherine Grainger: 5 medals (1 x Gold, 4 x Silver)

12. Steve Redgrave

13. Michael Phelps: 28 medals (23 x Gold, 3 x Silver, 2 x Bronze)

14. Greece – 1896

15. London 2012

16. 165,000

17. Blue, Yellow, Black, Green, Red *(along with the White Background, these colours were chosen as every nation's flag contains at least one of these colours)*

18. Baron Pierre de Coubertin

19. Five (Greece, Great Britain, France, Switzerland, Australia)

20. 13 years old 268 days; Marjorie Gestring (Diving – 1936 Olympics)

21. 1924

22. Norway: 132 Golds

23. Berlin 1936

24. Discus Throw

25. 100m Hurdles

26. James Cracknell, Steve Redgrave, Tim Foster, Matthew Pinsent

27. BMX Racing

28. Bolero

29. 120 metres

30. Lizzie Yarnold (Skeleton)

BASKETBALL

1. Barcelona 1992

2. Phil Jackson: Chicago Bulls (1989-98), LA Lakers (1999-2004, 2005-2011)

3. Wilt Chamberlain – 4,029 points (1961-62 season)

4. Kareem Abdul-Jabbar (38,387 points)

5. Boston Celtics

6. Minneapolis Lakers – 1948/49, 1949/50 (*Currently known as Los Angeles Lakers following a move to LA before the 1960/61 season*)

7. Cleveland Cavaliers

8. Miami Heat (2011/12, 2012/13)

9. Golden State Warriors, 73-9 (2015/16 season)

10. Andrew Bynum: drafted by LA Lakers in 2005 (17 years 249 days) and made his debut at 18 years and 6 days.

11. Michael Jordan (6)

12. 1996, selected by Charlotte Hornets

13. Bob Petit (1956, 1958, 1959, 1962)

14. Shaquille O'Neil

15. 45

16. New York Knicks

17. Boston Celtics: 8 times (1959-1966)

18. San Antonio Spurs

19. Michael Jordan; 63 points for Chicago Bulls vs Boston Celtics (1986)

20. Chase Center

BOXING

1. Rumble in the Jungle, Democratic Republic of Congo (Zaire)

2. Round 11 vs Technical Knockout

3. Undisputed Champion

4. Welterweight (140-147lbs)

5. Manny Pacquiao (Championships in Flyweight, Featherweight, Lightweight, and Welterweight divisions)

6. Muhammad Ali and Joe Frazier

7. Joe Calzaghe

8. Floyd Mayweather Jr. via Technical Knockout in the 10th round

9. 45 years old

10. Flyweight (Record: 6 fights, 5 wins, 1 draw)

11. Andy Ruiz Jr.

12. Athens 2004

13. Las Vegas, Nevada

14. Luke Campbell

15. Glasgow

16. Cruiserweight

17. Jake LaMotta

18. Cassius Marcellus Clay Jr.

19. Mike Tyson

20. 50-0 (27 KO)

CRICKET

1. Australia 21 – 15 England

2. Ravichandran Ashwin (54 Test Matches)

3. Brian Lara: 111 matches (*Tendulkar, Sangakkara, and Lara all reached milestones in the same number of Innings*)

4. 481 – *England* vs Australia (19th June 2018)

5. Sydney Sixers

6. Two Wickets (*Australia required 107 runs; England won by 2 runs*)

7. 17 balls

8. Eoin Morgan (95 matches, 2011-present), Jos Buttler (5 matches, 2016-2018), James Taylor (1 match, 2015)

9. Leicestershire: 3 times (2004, 2006, 2011)

10. Tammy Beaumont (410)

11. Pakistan, Sri Lanka, Australia

12. Jonny Bairstow – 150*

13. Rohit Sharma

14. Shakib Al Hasan

15. Michael Vaughan

16. 1882-83 (*in Australia*)

17. Ian Bell

18. Kings XI Punjab

19. Sachin Tendulkar & Rahil Dravid: 6,920 runs in 143 partnerships

20. Jofra Archer and Jos Buttler

CYCLING

1. 21 Stages

2. Individual Pursuit

3. Chris Hoy and Jason Kenny

4. Giro d'Italia, Tour de France, Vuelta a España

5. 1903

6. Yellow

7. Leader of the Young Rider Classification

8. Chris Froome

9. 3: *1986, 1989, 1990*

10. Mark Cavendish

11. Eddy Merckx: 11 (*5 x Tour de France, 5 x Giro, 1 x Vuelta*)

12. 2018 (Chris Froome - Giro; Geraint Thomas - Tour de France; Simon Yates – Vuelta)

13. Eight stages

14. The Monuments

15. Individual Sprint

16. Six (*2012, 13, 15, 16, 17, 18*)

17. Columbian

18. Italy – 52

19. North Yorkshire

20. Tony Rominger (1992, 93, 94)

DARTS

1. Alexander Palace (*'Ally Pally'*)
2. Michael Van Gerwen – 114.05 in 2017, Semi Final
3. Snakebite – Peter Wright
4. Fallon Sherrock
5. Eric Bristow
6. 170
7. 2018
8. Bobby George
9. 138
10. 1992
11. James Wade
12. Ladbrokes
13. John Part – 2003
14. Bullseye
15. Glen Durrant
16. Gerwyn Price
17. MvG: Michael Van Gerwen
18. Grand Slam of Darts
19. Russ Bray
20. Michael Smith

FOOTBALL

1. 90 + 4 minutes; Manchester City 3 -2 QPR

2. 1992-93, won by Manchester United

3. Arsenal, Chelsea, Everton, Liverpool, Manchester United, Tottenham Hotspur

4. Mario Götze

5. Gary Lineker (1986) and Harry Kane (2018)

6. Edwin Van Der Sar – 11 clean sheets (*2008/09 season*)

7. Sadio Mane, Mohamad Salah, Pierre-Emerick Aubameyang

8. Kepa (*Goalkeeper*): £72m. Harry Maguire (*Defender*): £80m. Philippe Coutinho (*Midfielder*): £105 million. Neymar (*Forward*): £198m

9. United States, Canada, Mexico

10. Celtic (1966/67)

11. Adidas Jabulani

12. Luis Suarez

13. Manchester City

14. Belgium

15. Nottingham Forest

16. Columbian

17. Sergio Roberto

18. Newcastle United

19. Mohamad Salah

20. Sam Allardyce (*Bolton Wanderers, Newcastle, Blackburn, West Ham, Sunderland, Crystal Palace, Everton*)

FORMULA ONE RACING

1. Red Bull

2. Damon Hill: 1996

3. Juan Manuel Fangio – 46 years old

4. Autodromo Nazionale Monza, Monza, Italy – 69 Grand Prix

5. Brawn

6. 2007

7. 1994

8. Haas F1 Team

9. McLaren

10. Germany

11. Alain Prost

12. 1982

13. Sebastian Vettel

14. Ferrari – 16

15. Fernando Alonso

16. Max Verstappen – 17 years and 180 days

17. Monaco

18. Abu Dhabi

19. Silverstone, Great Britain

20. Circuit Gilles-Villeneuve, Canada

GOLF

1. The Masters

2. Claret Jug

3. Bubba Watson

4. Masters Tournament

5. Francesco Molinari and Tommy Fleetwood

6. Brooks Koepka

7. Arnold Palmer

8. Augusta National Golf Club

9. Jason Day

10. 1987

11. Fijian

12. Justin Rose – U.S Open 2013

13. St. Andrews

14. Curtis Cup

15. Gary Player

16. Justin Rose

17. 14 ½

18. 14 clubs

19. Pádraig Harrington

20. Rickie Fowler (tied 5th at Masters, tied 2nd at U.S Open and Open Championship, and tied 3rd in PGA Championship)

HORSE RACING

1. Tiger Roll

2. Auroras Encore (66/1) and Mon Mome (100/1)

3. 1996

4. 201 metres

5. Native River

6. Aintree

7. Jonjo O'Neill

8. Eight winners

9. Donald "Ginger" McCain

10. Sandown Park

11. Nine times (*1954, '57, '60, '68, '70, '72, '76, '77, '83*)

12. Leighton Aspell

13. Pleasant Company

14. Pineau de Re (2014 Grand National Winner); sequence is Grand National Winners 2011, 2012, 2013, and 2014.

15. Derek Fox, One for Arthur, 2017

16. 2000 Guineas Stakes at Newmarket

17. Stradivarius

18. Thirty

19. Mite Bite

20. Randox Health

RUGBY UNION

1. England and Australia

2. Jason Robinson

3. Dan Carter (1,598)

4. Millenium Trophy

5. Wales – 4

6. Warren Gatland (Coach) & Sam Warburton (Captain)

7. France

8. New Zealand (1987, 2011) & South Africa (1995)

9. France

10. Wales, 19-16

11. Neil Jenkins

12. Bath

13. Exeter

14. 2002/03 season

15. Bath

16. Leicester Tigers (10 titles)

17. 2000, Italy

18. Sergio Parisse (69 appearances)

19. Guinness

20. Leinster and Toulouse

SNOOKER

1. Sheffield

2. Stephen Hendry – 7 times

3. Mark Williams

4. Neil Robertson

5. John Higgins, 18-14

6. Jimmy White

7. 2011/12 season

8. Joe Johnson

9. Terry Griffiths, 1979

10. Judd Trump

11. Canadian

12. 1981

13. 1991

14. 6 times

15. Betfred

16. 2013/14 season

17. World Championship, UK Championship, Masters

18. 2015

19. Ray Reardon

20. 33 frames; prior to 1997, was played over 31 frames

TENNIS

1. Martina Navratilova

2. Twelve

3. Milos Raonic

4. Heather Watson

5. Australian Open, 2008

6. 1998

7. Steffi Graf

8. Stan Wawrinka (2015) & Novak Djokovic (2016)

9. Romanian

10. Marin Čilić

11. 2009

12. Australian Open

13. Bob Bryan & Mike Bryan – 16 Grand Slams

14. 1877

15. Australian Open (mid-January)

16. Boris Becker & Stefan Edberg

17. Naomi Osaka

18. 1968, Rod Laver & Billie Jean King

19. Czech Republic

20. Andre Agassi completed the feat in 1999 by winning the French Open

TOP 10 ANSWERS

QUESTION ONE

1	United States	241
2	China	211
3	Russia	122
4	Great Britain	117
5	Germany	80
6	Australia	80
7	Japan	76
8	France	62
9	South Korea	58
10	Italy	57

QUESTION TWO

1	Eoin Morgan	210
2	Joe Root	158
3	Jos Buttler	157
4	Moeen Ali	121
5	Adil Rashid	113
6	Jason Roy	107
7	Chris Woakes	106
8	Ben Stokes	105
9	Jonny Bairstow	95
10	Ian Bell	82

QUESTION THREE

1	Manchester City	745
2	Chelsea	664
3	Arsenal	644
4	Tottenham Hotspur	640
5	Liverpool	625
6	Manchester United	594
7	Everton	503
8	West Ham United	367
9	Newcastle United	366
10	Stoke City	365

QUESTION FOUR

1	Emma Raducanu	2021
2	Lewis Hamilton	2020
3	Ben Stokes	2019
4	Geraint Thomas	2018
5	Sir Mo Farah	2017
6	Sir Andy Murray	2016, 2015, 2013
7	Lewis Hamilton	2014
8	Sir Bradley Wiggins	2012
9	Mark Cavendish	2011
10	Sir AP McCoy	2010

QUESTION FIVE

1	Steve Smith	(Aus) - 3044
2	Alistair Cook	(Eng) – 2493
3	Ricky Ponting	(Aus) – 2476
4	Steve Waugh	(Aus) – 2357
5	Michael Clarke	(Aus) – 2241
6	Mark Waugh	(Aus) – 2204
7	Kevin Pietersen	(Eng) – 2158
8	Joe Root	(Eng) – 2016
9	Ian Bell	(Eng) – 1983
10	David Warner	(Aus) - 1888

QUESTION SIX

1	Ryan Giggs	162
2	Cesc Fabregas	111
3	Wayne Rooney	103
4	Frank Lampard	102
5	James Milner	96
6	Dennis Bergkamp	94
7	David Silva	93
8	Steven Gerrard	92
9	Kevin De Bruyne	81
10	David Beckham	80

QUESTION SEVEN

1	Ben Youngs	115
2	Jason Leonard	114
3	Dylan Hartley	97
4	Dan Cole	95
5	Jonny Wilkinson	91
6	Courtney Lawes	91
7	Rory Underwood	85
8	Lawrence Dallaglio	85
9	Martin Johnson	84
10	Danny Care	84

QUESTION EIGHT

1	Shane Warne	(Aus) - 195
2	Glen McGrath	(Aus) – 157
3	Stuart Broad	(Eng) – 131
4	James Anderson	(Eng) – 112
5	Nathan Lyon	(Aus) – 101
6	Mitchell Johnson	(Aus) – 87
7	Peter Siddle	(Aus) – 80
8	Darren Gough	(Eng) – 74
9	Mitchell Starc	(Aus) – 74
10	Pat Cummins	(Aus) - 73

QUESTION NINE

1	Gareth Barry	653
2	Ryan Giggs	632
3	Frank Lampard	609
4	James Milner	589
5	David James	572
6	Gary Speed	535
7	Emile Heskey	516
8	Mark Schwarzer	514
9	Jamie Carragher	508
10	Phil Neville	505

QUESTION TEN

1	Rafael Nadal	22
2	Novak Djokovic	21
3	Roger Federer	20
4	Pete Sampras	14
5	Roy Emerson	12
6	Björn Borg	11
7	Rodney Laver	11
8	William Tilden	10
9	Frederick Perry	8
10	Andre Agassi	8

QUESTION ELEVEN

1	Serena Williams	23
2	Steffi Graf	22
3	Martina Navratilova	18
4	Chris Evert	18
5	Margaret Court	11
6	Monica Seles	9
7	Billie Jean King	8
8	Venus Williams	7
9	Evonne Goolagong Cawley	7
10	Justine Henin	7

QUESTION TWELVE

1	Brazil	73
2	Germany	67
3	Italy	45
4	Argentina	43
5	France	34
6	Spain	30
7	England	29
8	Netherlands	27
9	Uruguay	24
10	Sweden	19

QUESTION THIRTEEN

1	Yorkshire	33
2	Surrey	20
3	Middlesex	13
4	Lancashire	9
5	Warwickshire	8
6	Essex	8
7	Kent	7
8	Nottinghamshire	6
9	Worcestershire	5
10	Durham	3

QUESTION FOURTEEN

1	Michael Schumacher	7
2	Lewis Hamilton	7
3	Juan Manuel Fangio	5
4	Alain Prost	4
5	Sebastian Vettel	4
6	Jack Brabham	3
7	Jackie Stewart	3
8	Niki Lauda	3
9	Nelson Piquet	3
10	Ayrton Senna	3

QUESTION FIFTEEN

1	Jason Kenny	9 (7 x G, 2 x S)
2	Bradley Wiggins	8 (5 x G, 1 x S, 2 x B)
3	Chris Hoy	7 (6 x G, 1 x S)
4	Laura Kenny	6 (5 x G, 1 x S)
5	Steve Redgrave	6 (5 x G, 1 x B)
6	Charlotte Dujardin	6 (3 x G, 1 x S, 2 x B)
7	Max Whitlock	6 (3 x G, 3 x B)
8	Duncan Scott	6 (1 x G, 5 x S)
9	Ben Ainslie	5 (4 x G, 1 x S)
10	Jack Beresford	5 (3 x G, 2 x S)

QUESTION SIXTEEN

1	Real Madrid	14
2	Milan	7
3	Bayern	6
4	Liverpool	6
5	Barcelona	5
6	Ajax	4
7	Inter Milan	3
8	Manchester United	3
9	Chelsea	2
10	Porto	2

THE ULTIMATE SPORT QUIZ

QUESTION SEVENTEEN

1	Manchester United	20
2	Liverpool	19
3	Arsenal	13
4	Everton	9
5	Manchester City	8
6	Aston Villa	7
7	Chelsea	6
8	Sunderland	6
9	Sheffield Wednesday	4
10	Newcastle United	4

QUESTION EIGHTEEN

1	Athletics	55 Golds
2	Cycling	38 Golds
3	Rowing	31 Golds
4	Sailing	31 Golds
5	Swimming	20 Golds
6	Boxing	20 Golds
7	Tennis	17 Golds
8	Shooting	13 Golds
9	Equestrian	13 Golds
10	Canoeing	5 Golds

QUESTION NINETEEN

1	Wembley Stadium	90,000
2	Twickenham Stadium	82,000
3	Old Trafford	74,140
4	Millennium Stadium	73,971
5	Murrayfield Stadium	67,144
6	Tottenham Hotspur Stadium	62,850
7	London Stadium	62,500
8	Celtic Park	60,411
9	Emirates Stadium	60,260
10	Etihad Stadium	55,097

QUESTION TWENTY

1	Jack Nicklaus	6
2	Tiger Woods	5
3	Arnold Palmer	4
4	Phil Mickelson	3
5	Nick Faldo	3
6	Gary Player	3
7	Sam Snead	3
8	Jimmy Demaret	3
9	Bubba Watson	2
10	Jose Maria Olazabal	2

WORDSEARCHES

PAGE xx: Formula One Racing Teams

O	E	M	O	R	A	H	P	L	A			
							T					
		S	M	A	I	L	L	I	W			
	S	A	A	H			U					I
	E						A					R
		D					N					U
	L		E				E					A
	L		M	C	L	A	R	E	N			T
	U			R								A
	B				E							H
	D						M					P
	E											L
	R	A	C	I	N	G	P	O	I	N	T	A

PAGE xx: Netball Super League Teams

E	D	Y	L	C	H	T	A	R	T	S				
				E										H
				L										G
			R	T				S						U
			E	I		P								O
			T	C		S								R
			S	A	R	A	C	E	N	S				O
			E	W				U						B
			H				R			H				H
			C			R					T			G
			N		E							A		U
			A		Y								B	O
			M											L
		N	O	D	N	O	L							

PAGE xx: Golf Terms

					Y									
				E							R	A	P	
			G			R								
		O				E								
	B					T		Y						
		I				T		A						R
			R			U		W		E	L	G	A	E
				D		P		R						K
					I			I	E					N
N				H		E		A		V				U
E			C					F			I			B
E												R		
R		C	A	D	D	Y							D	
G														
							E	E	T					

PAGE xx: Premier League Top Scorers

			O	W	E	N							
E								D	R	A	P	M	A	L
O													
F		R	E	R	A	E	H	S					
E				O									
D					O								
				H	E	N	R	Y					
						E							
							Y						O
													R
		E											E
		L											U
		O			R	E	L	W	O	F			G
		C											A
				E	A	N	K						

PAGE xx: International Rugby Union Nations

	S	C	O	T	L	A	N	D			A	
											C	A
				D	N	A	L	E	R	I		N
									R			I
			A					F				T
W			I	E	N	G	L	A	N	D	E	N
A			L			H					C	E
L			A		T						N	G
E			R	U							A	R
S			T	O				N			R	A
			S					A			F	
			U							P		
			A								A	
	D	N	A	L	A	E	Z	W	E	N	J	

PAGE xx: GB Women's Hockey Starting Lineup Gold Medal Match 2016 Olympics

R		B	B	E	W		D	N	E	S	N	W	O	T
I	N						A							
C		E					N							
H			L				S							
A				L			O							
R						U	N	H						
D			E				C						H	
S			T		N								T	
O			I	I									R	
N			H					Y	A	R	B		O	
W			W					E					W	
A								L					S	
L								S					N	
S								N					U	
H			D	O	E	L	C	A	M					

PAGE xx: World Championship Snooker Winners

	E	B	D	O	N								
						M	A	H	G	N	I	B	
													N
S	N	I	G	G	I	H							O
													S
			P										T
N				M				T	T	O	D		R
A					U								E
V		Y				R							B
I	Y		H				T						O
L	B			P									R
L	L				R								
U	E					U							
S	S					S	M	A	I	L	L	I	W
O													

PAGE xx: Tennis Terms

				U										
				M	A	L	S	D	N	A	R	G		
			A	P				E						
		T		I					R					
	C			R						V				
H				E							E			
			L					K						
			L					A						
					A			E		S	E	T		
						B		R				R		
								B				U		
			T					E				O		
	E	C	U	E	D			I				C		
				N				T						

PAGE xx: Rugby Union Stadiums

		T	W	I	C	K	E	N	H	A	M		
E	M	O	R	D	O	L	E	V	E	D	A	T	S
C													S
N	M	U	R	R	A	Y	F	I	E	L	D		O
A	U												L
R	I			M	I	L	L	E	N	I	U	M	D
F	D			U									I
E	A				I								E
D	T					D							R
E	S		E	L	L	I	S	P	A	R	K		F
D	B								T				I
A	N									S			E
T	F										Z		L
S												N	D
O	C	I	P	M	I	L	O	O	I	D	A	T	S

PAGE xx: Artistic Gymnastic Disciplines

				M	A	E	B	E	C	N	A	L	A	B
E		S												
S		G										S		
R		N									R			
O		I								A	O			
H	O	R	I	Z	O	N	T	A	L	B	A	R		
L		L			R	O	O	L	F					
E		L			T		E							
M		I			L									
M		T			L		U							
O		S		A				A						
P			R					V						
		A						H						
		P	S	R	A	B	N	E	V	E	N	U		

PAGE xx: Golf Masters Winners

S	C	O	T	T								
			A	I	C	R	A	G				
											M	
										A		
		D							T			
	R	E	L	F	F	E	H	C	S			
		E					U					W
		R				Y					H	I
					A					T		L
N					M				E			L
O				A		S		I				E
S					D		P					T
T			J	O	H	N	S	O	N			T
A			O									
W		W										

PAGE xx: Rugby Positions

						W	O	R	D	N	O	C	E	S
	F					F								
	L	L				L								
	Y		A			A								
	H			N		H								T
	A				K	M							W	H
	L				E	U						I		G
	F				R	R					N			I
					T	C				G				E
					N	S			E					R
	P				E			R	E	K	O	O	H	E
	P				C									B
	R													M
	P													U
			K	C	A	B	L	L	U	F				N

PAGE xx: 1966 FIFA World Cup England Starting XI

S	R	E	T	E	P						L			
							S	E	L	I	T	S		
							A							
				N		B								
			E	R	O	O	M							
		H												
	O													
C														
H	U	N	T											
A						W								
R						I								
L						L								
T						S	K	N	A	B				
O						O								
N	C	H	A	R	L	T	O	N						

PAGE xx: Football Grounds

	V	I	C	A	R	A	G	E	R	O	A	D		
O							S			E				
L		K					E			N				
D		R	T				T			A				
T		A		U			A			L				D
R		P			R		R			L				A
A		T	K			F	I			L				O
F		S		R			M			A				R
F		R			A	O	E	O		M				W
O		U			L	P			O	A				O
R		H		I			A		O	R				R
D		L	N					L		B				R
		E						D	L	E	I	F	N	A
	U	S								I				C
X											V			

1. EMIRATES
2. VILLA PARK
3. TURF MOOR
4. SELHURST PARK
5. ANFIELD
6. OLD TRAFFORD
7. CARROW ROAD
8. BRAMALL LANE
9. VICARAGE ROAD
10. MOLINEUX

PAGE xx: England's 2019 Cricket World Cup Final Starting XI

				P	L	U	N	K	E	T	T		
				R									
				E									
		Y		H		N		T					
	W		O	C		A		O					
	O			R		G	O						
	T			A		R			D				
	S					O		I					
	R	E				M		H					
	I		K				S						
	A			A		A		E					
	B				O	R			K		D		
					W					O			
									O		T		
	R	E	L	T	T	U	B		W				S

1. Jason **ROY**
2. Jonathan **BAIRSTOW**
3. Joe **ROOT**
4. Eoin **MORGAN**
5. Ben **STOKES**
6. Jos **BUTTLER**
7. Chris **WOAKES**
8. Liam **PLUNKETT**
9. Jofra **ARCHER**
10. Adil **RASHID**
11. Mark **WOOD**

HARD: Heptathlon Events

Find the seven events in a Heptathlon in the Wordsearch below…

		L				T	U	P	T	O	H	S		
			O								E			
			N						L					
				G				D						8
					J		R							0
						U								0
					H		M							M
N					M			P						R
	I			0										U
		L	0											N
		1	E		2	0	0	M	R	U	N			
				V										
				A										
			P	M	U	J	H	G	I	H				

1. 100M HURDLES
2. HIGH JUMP
3. SHOT PUT
4. 200M RUN

5. LONG JUMP
6. JAVELIN
7. 800M RUN

HARD: American Football Team Names

Complete the following NFL Team names and find the Nickname in the wordsearch below...

	S											
	E											
	A			C	O	W	B	O	Y	S		
	H											
	A				S	S			S			
	W				N	T		L	T	R		
S	K		S		I	N		A	O		A	
T	S		N		K	A	N		I		E	
E			O		S	I			R			B
E			C		D	G			T			
L			L	R	E				A			
E			A		R				P			
R		C	F									
S												
		S	E	L	G	A	E					

1. *Arizona* CARDINALS
2. *Atlanta* FALCONS
3. *Chicago* BEARS
4. *Dallas* COWBOYS
5. *New England* PATRIOTS
6. *New York* GIANTS
7. *Philadelphia* EAGLES
8. *Pittsburgh* STEELERS
9. *Seattle* SEAHAWKS
10. *Washington* REDSKINS

HARD: Previous 10 England Football Team Managers

*Find the Surnames of the last 10 England Football Managers
(hint: First names provided) ...*

N					N		N	E	R	A	L	C	C	M
O					A									
S					G									
S		S			E	C	R	A	E	P				
K			O		E									
I				U	K									N
R					T	A	Y	L	O	R				O
E						H								S
					O		G							N
				D			C	A	P	E	L	L	O	I
			G						T					K
		S								E				L
	O													I
N														W
	A	L	L	A	R	D	Y	C	E					

1. *Gareth* SOUTHGATE
2. *Sam* ALLARDYCE
3. *Roy* HODGSON
4. *Stuart* PEARCE
5. *Fabio* CAPELLO

6. *Steve* MCCLAREN
7. *Sven-Göran* ERIKSSON
8. *Peter* TAYLOR
9. *Kevin* KEEGAN
10. *Howard* WILKINSON

HARD: IPL Cricket Teams

Find the Eight Cities that are home to these IPL Teams
(hint: Franchise name is provided)...

I	A	B	M	U	M						D			
											A			
N											B			
A											A			
H					C			B			R		A	
T						H		A			E		T	
S							E	J			D		A	
A		I						N			Y		K	
J		H						U	N		H		L	
A		L						P		A			O	
R		E									I		K	
		D												
	E	R	O	L	A	G	N	A	B					

1. CHENNAI *Super Kings*	9. MUMBAI *Indians*
2. DELHI *Capitals*	10. RAJASTHAN *Royals*
3. PUNJAB *Kings*	11. *Royal Challengers* BANGALORE
4. KOLKATA *Knight Riders*	12. *Sunrisers* HYDERABAD

HARD: Summer and Winter Olympic Host Cities

Find the 10 host cities of the Summer and Winter Olympics between 2000-2018 (hint: Country provided) ...

		Y	T	I	C	E	K	A	L	T	L	A	S
						N	O	D	N	O	L		
	S	Y	D	N	E	Y							
O													
R			G	G									
I				N									
E		R		I	A			I					
N		E		J		H		H					
A		V		I			C						
J		U		E		O		G			A		
E		O		B	S				N		T		
D		C							I	O	H		
O		N							R		E		
I		A							U		N	Y	
R		V							T		S		P

1. PYEONGCHANG
2. RIO DE JANEIRO
3. SOCHI
4. LONDON
5. VANCOUVER

6. BEIJING
7. TURIN
8. ATHENS
9. SALT LAKE CITY
10 SYDNEY

Printed in Great Britain
by Amazon

15371727R00112